Coaching Fastpitch Softball:

Championship Drills, Tips, and Insights

By:

JERRAD HARDIN

10-Digit ISBN 1-59113-934-1
13-Digit ISBN 978-1-59113-934-8

Printed in the United States of America.

ChampionshipFastpitch.com
2006

Acknowledgments

I would like to acknowledge my editor, Steve Lebedz, for his wonderful work and encouragement, Glenn Moore for writing the foreword and being a faithful contributor, Terry Graver for his friendship and willingness to help, Janice Esses, Tom Spencer, Ed Lantzer, Scott Howard, Amie Stewart, Amy Hayes, Heinz Mueller, Keith Hauber, Dave Johnson, Natalie Poole, and George Jones for all of their valuable time and professional insights.

I give special thanks to God, my family, and friends. Thank you for always believing in me. Hannah, I love you, thanks for being my inspiration.

Contents

About Jerrad Hardin

- **2002-2003** *Nebraska Coaches Association Coach of the Year*
- **181-77** *Career Record*
- *Inherited a Cozad team that was 7-21, the first year his team finished 17-14 and district runner-up, followed by five straight trips to the state tournament.*

    - *1999 State Runner-up*
    - *2001 State Champion*
    - *2002 State Champion*

- ***12** players have moved on to play in college--3 Division I--1 NCAA Division I All-American*

State Class Team Records:

- *Most Runs Scored in a Season -* ***266***
- *Most Hits in as Season -* ***378***
- *Most Doubles in a Season -* ***46***
- *Most Triples in a Season -* ***30***

State Class Individual Records:

- *Most Runs Scored in a Season -* ***48***
- *Most Runs Scored in a Career -* ***138***
- *Hits in a Season -* ***64***
- *Hits in a Career -* ***190***
- *Consecutive Games with a Hit -* ***23***
- *RBI in a season (All-Class Record) -* ***49***
- *Doubles in a Game -* ***3***
- *Triples in a Season (All-Class Record) -* ***11***
- *Triples in a Career (All-Class Record) -* ***23***
- *Stolen Bases in a Season (All-Class Record)* ***67***

- *Stolen Bases in a Career (All-Class Record)* ***153***

- *Lowest Earned Run Average for a Season -* ***0.08 , 0.26, 0.43*** *(Three Listings)*

Total - ***19,*** *Team & Individual State Records*

- ***44*** *1st Team, 2nd Team, Honorable Mention, and Academic All-State Recipients*
- ***19*** *First Team All-State Selections*
- *Engineered a* ***$50,000*** *fund-raising effort to renovate the CHS softball program.*
- *Teams set nearly every school record in every conceivable category at two different schools.*
- *Led Bellevue West to its first tournament win, and most victories in a season.*
- *Guided Bellevue West to its* ***1st top 10*** *ranking, and finished in the* ***top 10*** *for the first time in school history.*
- ***6*** *of* ***8*** *teams coached finished the season in the* ***top 10****. Only exceptions were the first year at each school.*

While all these facts and figures are impressive on their own, they may mean very little to people outside of Nebraska softball. What is most significant, I think, is that Coach Hardin has consistently produced quality programs and individuals. I have worked around numerous coaches in my 32-year career as a teacher/coach, but Jerrad Hardin possesses the most knowledge of his sport of anyone I have been around. Many coaches are great practice coaches or great game day coaches; Coach Hardin is the whole package. It has been a tremendously fun learning experience just working alongside him each day. His practices are organized to the minute, and every minute has a purpose for that day. Coaches of all levels of experience can learn from this book.

~ Steve Lebedz, Assistant Coach

Foreword

It was 6 pm on a typical hot, humid day in the rural southern Mississippi community of East Fork. The East Fork "Coon Hunters," the team my dad and two older brothers played for and another local team were warming up to play a game of softball. We didn't call it fastpitch softball because if men played softball in those days it was fastpitch. Slow-pitch was played only by the women and girls. Softball was the favorite past time back then.

I was only the batboy but I loved the game as much as the men who actually played it. I was twelve years old and one of five boys in our family of seven children and I knew that one day I would get "called up" from bat boy and the cup ball leagues to play with the men; I just didn't know it would be *this* day.

It was not unusual for a team to have only seven or eight players show up, but there were always older guys, who had come just to watch, willing to fill in. This day was not unlike the others except for the fact that rather than choosing one of those guys to fill in, my Dad, a great pitcher; revered by all and a man among men to me, PICKED ME! "Glenn, you play right field," my dad said. In a sudden state of shock but not about to question the greatest pitcher I had ever seen, I, wearing a t-shirt, a pair of cut off blue jean shorts and no shoes, ran straight to the position they always put the worst player on the team- *without a glove*! I got a glove from an opponent who would be playing the same position the next half of the inning and went on to play in my very first fastpitch softball game. It was that single moment that sparked what would become an intense lifelong passion for the game I am so indebted to today.

Through the years few things in life have given me as much satisfaction as passing along the enjoyment I have had to the young athletes who share the same passion. Almost everything I know about softball I learned from someone else, whether it was my dad or a twelve year old at one of our camps. This game has advanced and is much more technical than it was in those days, largely because of the willingness of coaches and players to share information. This book is about just that – sharing information. It contains information and philosophies of people who share the same love of the game and, if applied, this book will positively change your game forever. Make sure you share what you learn from it with someone else.

Glenn Moore
Baylor University

Introduction

It's the third inning already, and we're leading our opponent by five runs in the state championship game. I'm quite comfortable that my pitcher and defense have all the run support that they are going to need.

After all, we ended up outscoring our opponents in post-season play 42-1. The numbers are misleading, though, because it's never that easy. As I sat there in the dugout perched upon my stool, I began to reminisce about all the hard work and sacrifices that everyone had made for us to get to this particular moment. How players begged for extra repetitions, parents supported pitching and hitting lessons, assistant coaches unselfishly lent their time, and how I spent every available moment thinking of ways to make our program better. Most of my days were occupied sketching out practice plans between classes and searching the internet during my planning period for fastpitch articles to better my knowledge. Then at night I would re-evaluate our most recent practice over a microwave dinner before turning to a book about coaching or watching a video about how to do it better.

Sitting unusually calm and collected, I noticed the game began to take a backseat to the memories that had led me to this enviable spot. Unbeknownst to any observer, as I continued to call pitches, my attention was somewhat divided. Astonishingly enough, my memories took me back to the first game that I had coached. It was also the first fastpitch softball game I had ever seen. We got beat by the ten-run rule, and I'm quite sure it looked as though I knew nothing about what I was doing. And I have to confess that I really didn't.

That moment lives in sharp contrast to how we ended that season. Relying on a talented freshman and several upper-classmen full of potential, we shocked our opposition by making it to the district finals before losing, 2-0. It was the first winning season in the short history of the program. For most teams a season ending with a 17-14 record would be fairly unceremonious. However, it served as a launching point for our program which had managed a meager 7-21 finish the previous year.

That finish alone propelled our kids into believing they could achieve more. It was an internal motivation that seemed to be contagious among all of the players. We finished our season that year in October, and began working in groups of four again by mid-November. Unselfishly and relentlessly, those kids worked from November to August, never complaining and without ever losing sight of their goal to participate in the state tournament the following season.

It just so happened, their commitment paid off. The following season, our kids willed themselves to the state tournament and finished in the championship game. Despite losing in the championship game we had exceeded everyone's expectations by making it to the finals as the lowest seed in the field. The loss did little to dampen our spirits, as we worked even harder during the next off-season in hopes of turning our silver medals into gold.

The following year we found ourselves back at the state tournament, but, handicapped with hardships and injuries, we fell short of our goal. A two-time state qualifier now, we began to expect nothing less than an annual trip. Also, after failing twice to bring back a state championship, our returning players became ever-more-motivated to do whatever they had to in order to win it all. I was equally motivated to become a better coach; therefore, I attended more clinics, developed new charts, and devoted more time to scouting our opposition.

As the championship game progresses, I find myself relaxing with an unfamiliar demeanor. We're in complete control and on the verge of winning the state championship. It would be the first softball state championship for our school. And oddly enough, I felt more at ease than in any other game I had ever coached. What an odd paradox. The biggest game of my life and I'm more relaxed than I've ever been.

Immersed in my own world, I'm simply enjoying the moment. As the innings slowly play out, memories continue to saturate my thinking. And with every out, there is a glow that continues to illuminate every standing body in our dugout. The kids can certainly feel what is about to happen; it's evident as their faces struggle to fight back a flood of premature emotions. I could only hope that they would remember this moment as vividly as I hoped to.

It was the seventh inning. We were in control with a commanding lead of 7-0. With two outs, our opponent managed to get a base runner to third on back-to-back errors. Obviously, it was becoming increasingly difficult for our team to stay focused with the undeniable jubilation that was waiting to explode. Instinctively, it was at that moment that I snapped out of my trance and swiftly made my way onto the field to visit with the team. My approach was intense and focused. I started coaching again. I'm not even sure my team was even listening to what I was barking, as they just looked at me, and said, "It'll be alright, Coach."

Sure enough, they were right; the next pitch produced an out, and we were state champions.

It is hard to predict how one will react in that situation. There is nothing premeditated. The celebration is unscripted and uncontrollable with kids hugging, crying, and dancing around with excitement. In contrast, as a coach, I felt emotionally paralyzed, unable to express any of the emotion that I had been harboring throughout the contest. Perhaps it was the unlikelihood of the situation considering where we started from, or maybe it's just a crippling feeling of relief from high expectations of a program on the brink.

I had written the above passage a few days after winning the first of back-to-back state championships as a high school fastpitch softball coach. At the time, it was my intent to capture the emotion and feelings of the moment so that I could remember it forever. The truth is, it wasn't something I would have had to document to relive. Such a memory is what many of us dream of, strive for, and prepare for.

Creating a successful fastpitch softball program requires hard work, dedication, and direction. The amount of time and commitment you invest will ultimately be your decision. However, you can be assured that this publication will provide you with invaluable tips, drills, and insights to take your team to the next level. Over a dozen fastpitch coaches, from every level, across the country, have contributed key elements. You'll find ideas from how to form a basic philosophy to how to motivate your team. In addition, you'll find practice ideas, position-by-position breakdowns, special situation plays, game-planning reminders, and much more. Good luck and hopefully you'll find this book to be a useful guide in your quest for success.

Chapter 1

Creating a Philosophy

If you stay around in coaching long enough, your philosophy is bound to change. It's okay, don't cringe; that statement wasn't written to scare you. It doesn't mean that how you handle your athletes, approach the game, and, ultimately, how you coach is necessarily wrong, nor does it mean that someday a little light will come on and you'll suddenly have it all figured out. It simply means that as time passes, your philosophy on coaching will change, if not evolve with gained knowledge. I can assure you if you are a first-year coach or a seasoned veteran, certain elements concerning your overall philosophy will change.

Ten years ago I wrote a philosophy paper for my Coaching Theory class while in college. I pulled it out a few years back to see how my philosophy had changed.

Wow...

As I read through the mangled mess, my stomach turned, not only at the thoughts I had represented in my writing but at the boldness with which I proclaimed to set the world on fire with my superhuman coaching powers. Needless to say a few disappointing losses and the reality of the coaching world changed my philosophy immensely.

Although I have been flexible and allowed myself to evolve and adjust with each passing season, I do remain true to my ***fundamental beliefs for success:***

1. Keep it Simple

2. Have Commitment

3. Demonstrate Selflessness

4. Always Be Disciplined

Whatever your fundamental philosophy is, stick true to the basis of your beliefs; however, be willing to change with every learned experience to suit the ever-changing climate of your athletes and the environment you work in. Coach Tom Spencer, currently at Notre Dame College in South Euclid, Ohio, sums it up best with his approach to his coaching philosophy: *"My philosophy may change every year based upon the makeup of my team. But overall we try to keep it simple. We preach attitude and effort. If our players have a great attitude and always give 100% effort we feel we will be successful."*

Different Philosophies

Scott Howard, Liberty H.S. – Liberty, MO

My philosophy is two-fold. First, everyone involved has to believe in the program, the system, the coaches, and the players. Secondly, as a coach, you have to be able to pass the leadership to the players. In some seasons, it may happen more naturally or quickly than others, but it has to happen.

Janice Esses / Bethany College – Lindsborg, KS

I care for each of my players. I don't just care about them as a player, but also as a student and person. I think it is my responsibility to help them reach their potential as a player, help them graduate and achieve their goals in life. As coaches, we are not only teachers of our sport, but we are also teachers of life. I feel that if I show my players that I care for them, when I get on them for making mistakes, they will know that I am only helping them get better and that I still care for them.

Heinz Mueller, Phoenix College / NJCAA – Phoenix, AZ

Keep the game simple, recruit talented athletes and have a great coaching staff that is very loyal and hardworking. Last is, make the game fun and attractive to players so that they can hardly wait to play the game.

Glenn Moore, Baylor University – Waco, TX

Aggressive play utilizing a balance between the short game and power. Motivate players through fun competition. Play the percentages and make the basic plays.

Mission Statements

Businesses, schools, and organizations are great for creating ***mission statements***. Why not create one for your team that reflects your philosophy? Put it on your letterhead, handbooks, or at the bottom of your signature line on your email. Making it visible helps market your program and your beliefs.

Every season I try to do this. I take my philosophy of coaching and paraphrase it so that my ideas can be concisely conveyed to my audience, which generally consists of my administration, players and their parents.

Write down your basic coaching philosophy. Then ask yourself three questions:

- What do I want to accomplish?
- What do I want the team to achieve?

- How will we accomplish these goals?

As an example, take a look below at Elkhorn High School Coach Terry Graver's basic philosophy and notice how it easily serves as a ***mission statement***.

Basic Philosophy: Making softball fun while expecting and demanding a lot from our players.

Would you agree that Coach Graver's basic philosophy would serve as a powerful mission statement?

Don't underestimate how important communicating your philosophy can be. Showing a steady belief in your approach to the game is perhaps one of the best things that you can do whether you are a novice coach or a long-time veteran. Illustrating this tells everyone what you're all about while also providing a clear direction for your team to follow.

"Work hard, but enjoy what you do." ~ Keith Hauber, Lake Central H.S.

Chapter 2

Program Building

"I feel a good barometer for any program is the number of student athletes that are coming out for your sport. If you have a good thing going, most kids want to be a part of it. Because of our recent success, our numbers have increased each year. If your athletes are having fun and enjoying a little bit of success, other kids notice that and want to be a part of it as well."

~ Ed Lantzer, Lake H.S., Uniontown, OH

Whether you are taking over a new program or trying to rejuvenate a struggling program, this section should be helpful to you. I've been fortunate enough to have been a part of both. While in Cozad, the program was relatively new – only in its third year but we were able to turn our tiny program into one of Nebraska's best. Then at Bellevue West our staff was able to turn around a program that had struggled since its inception more than a decade earlier. Both experiences were equally positive and eerily similar in the approach that was taken.

New Programs

When taking over a new program, it's important to tame your expectations but never your enthusiasm. Luck will play a part with the hand you are dealt, but there is no substitute for a relentless work ethic if you want long-term success with your program.

In Cozad, I benefited from a strong summer youth program that had been in place several years before my arrival as the high school coach. One of the first steps you should take is to find out the names of the coaches who run the community's youth teams and immediately introduce yourself. You will find that, in most cases, you will have instant credibility with these coaches and many will see you as an expert. A large number of community youth coaches are comprised of parents and, believe it or not, most will be receptive to your input.

You shouldn't underestimate the importance of these youth programs. They will serve as the developmental stages of your program. It's almost like the farm system that Major League Baseball uses. And unmistakably, it's the teams that possess the best farm systems such as the Atlanta Braves who will endure long-lasting success. Creating your own well-managed developmental program will establish long-term success for your program.

Terry Graver, Elkhorn H.S., Elkhorn NE

For us the youth is a huge factor from ages 4-12. I am a board member of the youth program and have a hands-on-approach. Many of our players move into Omaha to play on select teams after age 14. We are lucky; Omaha teams play at a high level and many of our players make those teams.

Introducing Yourself to Youth Coaches

It's important that, even though they may view you as an expert, you don't initially come across as such. Youth coaches will not want to be overwhelmed by your treasure of knowledge during the first meeting. This can push them away from you, and you want them on your side. Building a cooperative partnership with them will allow your techniques and teaching methods to be filtered down to the youngest group. This not only benefits your program but it also gives consistent instruction to the kids involved.

Invite your youth coaches to your practices and allow them to see how hard you work and your level of instruction. By doing so, they are more likely to adopt some of your drills and perhaps even your mannerisms. I keep all of my practices open; there's really nothing to hide – if you're a coach don't be afraid to let people see what you do!

In keeping with your relationship with your youth coaches, ask to attend one of their practices. The kids will be excited to see the high school coach present, and you may be surprised at just how much of your teaching you see the youth coaches implementing. I only wish I had a win for every time I heard a youth coach say, "When you get to high school, Coach Hardin is going to expect…."

Maintaining the Relationship

It doesn't stop with introducing yourself and giving youth coaches a free pass to your practices. You should make every opportunity to make them feel a part of your program. Don't shy away from inviting them to banquets, fundraisers, and even some team-related activities. Include them in your camps and clinics and call upon them whenever you need help putting on a tournament. These people will be invaluable patrons for your program and can act as a voice of support that rings throughout the community when things aren't going well for your team.

Publicly acknowledge the importance of the community's youth program to your high school team's success and see your program grow. There are several outlets in which this can be done:

- Banquets
- Newspaper Interviews
- Conversations with Patrons
- Websites
- Banners
- Newsletters

Meeting the Team

First impressions can be lasting. Unless you've been coaching for a long period or you've gained a reputation through success like Heinz Mueller, of Phoenix College, who owns 650 career victories and four national championships, then you need to establish your expectations from day one. For most of us our reputation fails to precede us; therefore, be prepared before you meet your team.

It's important when you meet your team for the first time that you demonstrate to them that you are organized, enthusiastic, and committed. You can't put enough paper in their hands: guidelines, expectations, parent letters, schedules, personal contact information.

Also, we pass out a *questionnaire* to every prospective player. The reason I do this is simple: I want to find out who they are and what their expectations are. The questions are fairly general, but they reveal so much about my players. I not only find out their contact information, but also how they perceive their own abilities, the latter of which can be extremely useful when managing players.

Distributing information and being prepared are certainly important elements to any first meeting; however, above all, remember to be you. If you act as if you are someone that you really are not, then it won't take your team long to figure that out. With them doing so, you will quickly prove to be inconsistent and possibly lose credibility with your athletes.

If you are nervous, that's normal. After all, the young ladies you're introducing yourself to will be judging you. That's why it is important to go into the meeting prepared and organized; it will help you with your confidence, which is vital. Your team will likely adopt your mannerisms and beliefs. You want your team to be confident, not cocky, but without a doubt, absolutely sure of themselves. You want to establish this persona or at least lay the groundwork for it from day one.

Think about it, who are the best teams in your area? What demeanor do they have when they take the field? Do they reflect the attitudes of their coach?

In the 2002 State Tournament we were heavily favored to repeat within our class. The second game of the tournament, we lost 1-0. Our kids were crushed; we found ourselves in unfamiliar territory and we were only one loss away from going home empty-handed. We played an elimination game later that evening and narrowly escaped. I could see our team was a little back on their heels – as was I - therein lay the problem. I met with my coaches at the hotel later that evening prior to our team meeting. We talked about the importance of regaining our confidence and swagger before competing the next day. In order to repeat, we would have to play four games; seven in two days. In addition, our all-state pitcher's back was shot, so she was going to be limited, and that definitely wasn't helping our confidence.

In our meeting I spoke with great conviction. Whether or not I actually believed we could accomplish the feat before us, I displayed zero doubt. Players began standing up in the crowded room, one by one, each expressing their confidence. I hardly recognized my own team the next day. They were on a mission, focused beyond anything I had ever seen before and it was obvious in their intensity and approach to each game. This isn't a great mystery novel; we won all four games that day and got stronger and more convincing with each victory.

The following year at the banquet that precedes the state tournament I bumped into the coach who our team had beaten twice in the finals to win the 2002 championship. He told me that our kids had a fire in their eyes that night and he knew immediately that we wouldn't be denied. Confidence can be intimidating, but it has to be instilled and exemplified by your coaching staff.

My grandpa used to tell me, "Never let 'em see ya sweat." I've always tried to apply this to any situation where I have to talk in front of any group of people. The instructions are simple and pragmatic, but they can also be empowering. **Translation:** *You are the expert, you are the one in control, and your audience is at your mercy; therefore, don't let them think anything different by letting them see you sweat!*

Tip: Things to Consider When Meeting Your Team

- Be Confident
- Be Prepared
- Be Organized
- Be Yourself

Off-Season Programs

Being involved with your community's youth program will benefit you for long-term success, but a meaningful *off-season program* can bring immediate improvements. In Cozad, our team improved from 17-14 in year one to 24-8 and state runner-up the following season. At Bellevue West, our team went from 12-13 in our first year to a top ten finish, and a 22-12 record the very next.

I attribute both examples to the work we did in the time spent between our seasons. Your players will ultimately determine the success of any program you choose to implement. However, it is up to you to sell it to your team and encourage them to participate. When considering any off-season plan, you need to first identify your team's needs. By pinpointing your areas of improvement you can maximize your efforts.

There are many different off-season programs that you can purchase. There is also an abundance of information that you can obtain by just asking. You'll find that many high school and collegiate coaches are willing to share their ideas.

Whatever you choose to do, a good place to start is by implementing a consistent and well-developed weight training regimen. Building a strong central core will increase the strength of your players as well as help prevent sports-related injuries. Again, you can consult a number of other coaches to find out what they do. However, don't hesitate to use the experts within your own building if you are a high school coach. It's been my experience that weight-training coaches are more than willing to help construct routines that will develop overall athleticism. Local hospitals often have athletic trainers and physical therapists who can also aid in the process.

We had the good fortune at Cozad to have a local physical therapist who was extremely supportive of our high school athletic programs. She conducted a stretching clinic on our first day of conditioning that we benefited from everyday for the rest of the season. She would also stop out at our field before practice at the beginning of each week to make sure everything was going well. This sort of support and involvement can create in-roads for you that can benefit your program in many different ways.

During our last off-season I consulted with several individuals before starting an *18-week lifting and conditioning routine* that I picked up from a friend who was once in the Anaheim Angels organization. It was a great workout book, but obviously it wasn't designed specifically for fastpitch or for female athletes. Working with our weight-training coaches, a trainer, and others, we were able to revamp it and put together a comprehensive workout plan that significantly improved our team's athleticism. The weight-training coaches were also more than happy to allow my players (whom they had in their classes) to do our specific workout.

Tip: Things to Remember Before Beginning Any Lifting Program

- Get the Approval of Your Administration
- Involve Experts Within Your Environment
- Consult With Other Coaches
- Be Aware of Any Physical Limitations or Special Needs
- Sell it To Your Players
- Create a Time that Works for Your Athletes

Raising Expectations

Expectations and goals work in conjunction with one another; however, they are different. Your expectations are what you expect from your team, while your goals are what you wish to achieve. You can't have one work well without the other. Expectations will provide a standard from which to work, and your goals are what your team will be working for. Who wants to work up to high expectations if there isn't anything to work for? Furthermore, who can achieve goals without any basis to operate from?

Expectations need to be thoughtful, fair, and consistent. It's not wrong to provide lofty expectations, but be cautious not to burn your team out with overzealous ideas. It's best to create expectations that can be regularly met. This provides your team with a sense of accomplishment as they work toward their goals. If they constantly fall short of your expectations, then a pessimistic feeling may develop, almost like a "why even try" attitude. This is not the direction you want your team to go, so temper your expectations and make them challenging yet attainable.

What should you expect from your team? If your expectations are too low, will your team ever meet their potential? What if your expectations are too high and your team consistently falls short? There are many things to consider when setting expectations for your personnel including: history, character, and commitment.

History

If you are new to a program, do your homework and find out what the history of the program has been. Find out if they've been successful or if they perennially fail. This information will allow you to appropriately set expectations. Find out how the previous coach ran practices. This will provide you with an understanding of how receptive players may initially be to your style.

Determine who your allies and enemies might be. Where can you turn for unbiased opinions and needed advice? There will be times when you need outside resources. Are there people that you should avoid? Some people may pretend to be helpful but are eventually the ones that stab you in the back. You need to find out who those people are before you get a knife stuck in between your shoulder blades.

Having knowledge of your program will allow you to set appropriate expectations for your team. Knowing how things have been done in the past can serve you well in how you talk to your team, ask for favors, and push your kids on a daily basis. Talking to your athletic director, your team, and even an unbiased observer will generate a base of information. How you then use it is up to you. After all, you are the one who has to make the final decision as to what to expect from your team.

Character

Discover the character of your team before revealing your expectations. This is done usually within the first week of conditioning. Observe their attitudes when you make them run an extra sprint. Do they balk at the idea? Do they embrace the challenge? How they react can speak volumes about their character, regarding what you expect.

And if their verbal or non-verbal expressions lead you to believe that they are dissatisfied with your instructions, then you know how your expectations are affecting them. So how should you handle this? Some coaches might suggest that the team will have to rise to the expectations set forth. We believe that in doing so a gap between players and coaches may develop. Instead, find out through conversation what your players want to accomplish and then become a salesperson convincing them of what has to be done in order to achieve *their goals.*

Character can be changed. However, it won't change unless you can open a line of communication with your players that convinces them to meet your expectations that coincide with their goals. There isn't a certain timetable for this to occur. Some teams will take it on immediately while others will continually reject it. Sooner or later, the expectations won't be solely yours, but they will belong to your team.

Commitment

How committed your team is, and the number who are fully committed, will set the standard for what to expect for the future. If your team puts forth the hard work and determination to succeed, it will set the bar high. Teams that follow will inherently be expected to reach that level. This happens in programs all across America in schools that have won multiple state championships. It seems as though every year those teams simply reload and compete year in and year out. It's their commitment to the expectations that have previously been set that continue to drive them.

How much will your kids do in the off-season? How many hours will they spend in the weight room or batting cage? Will they attend camps and clinics? If you expect them to do these things and they are willing to do them, then you will establish a commitment that lives long after your initial efforts. It's almost like physically constructing something that lives long after the labor put forth to build it.

Having a group of committed kids will reflect your program's expectations. The question is always how we get our kids to make such commitment. We believe that starts with finding out where they want to go. Open a line of communication with your team and honestly talk about where they are now and where they want to be. From this, develop clear goals and then show them how your expectations will help make their dreams come true.

Goal-Setting

Every season on the first day we meet I ask my athletes to tell me what their goal is for the season. Every season, I get a similar response, "Go to state!" I'm assuming that is an answer that most of you would be familiar with. After all, who doesn't want to participate in the state tournament?

Goals are easy to measure. You either achieve them, or you don't. Because of this, it is best to understand the psyche of your team before setting forth any goals. What will happen if they fail to meet their goals? Will they embrace the challenge of meeting all their goals? Are the goals provided realistic? Are they unreachable? There are many questions that should be answered before developing goals. Sometimes it can be helpful if you ask your team first.

We think it's important to involve your team when making decisions about what they wish to accomplish. You may be surprised at what they come up with. Kids are inventive and creative, and when you involve them in this process, you'll quickly learn that. Not every idea they provide will be useful. One particular player, when asked to outline goals for the season, responded with the following:

Goal #1 – To work hard enough to get doughnuts before every morning practice.

Goal #2 – Become closer by having team dinners before every tournament.

Goal #3 – Show more togetherness by eating with each other at lunch.

(This came from one of our seniors and she was serious – and evidently not fed well at home.)

Regardless of what they come up with, you have to know that your team will feel empowered by the process, and they will likely put forth more effort in trying to reach goals they have set. We use a process that allows us to democratically set forth goals. Then after setting goals we talk about what the expectations should be for us to achieve them. This is a healthy conversation that draws everyone in and brings everyone onto the same page.

The process is simple and can take as little as 20 minutes, depending on how many kids you involve. I usually do this only with our varsity team which generally numbers between 14-16 kids. We meet as a group in a classroom and I explain the general idea of what we're trying to achieve. It's then that I ask them to privately write down three goals that they have for the team. Then they take turns orally presenting their ideas to the group. After each submission the team votes with a show of hands as to which idea they like the most. It's then recorded on the chalkboard for everyone to see. By the time you get to the last person, there will have been several repeats. In all, we might have ten or twelve ideas on the board. We then vote to identify the five or six they feel are the most important. I really try to merely facilitate the process. My input is minimal and serves mainly as directional. Therefore, when it's all done, the team has created its own set of goals.

When their goals have been identified, I type them out and print a copy to be signed by each coach and teammate. From that I make a dozen or so copies and make sure each player gets one. We discuss their goals and talk about what we should expect from ourselves to achieve them. This gives the coaching staff ammunition to fire at them in practice when they are under-achieving. We constantly remind them of their goals and what they need to do to reach them. And because they are their own set of goals, they respond better when coaches raise expectations.

Tip: Coach Natalie Poole on Goal-Setting

Goal-setting can be a challenging task. I have done quite a bit of reading and researching on the process of goal-setting. I have found some great information in two books written by Jeff Janssen, M.S. They are ***The Team Captain's Leadership Manual*** ***and*** ***Championship Team Building.*** *We follow along with many of the things that he suggests to do when setting goals. We begin with first coming up with a mission for the year. The way that we determine the mission is to separate the team into three groups with equal representation of upperclassmen with underclassmen. We have each group come up with ideas for the mission based on what we would like to achieve in the season if we really put our hearts and minds into it.*

We will come back together and share what they have listed and why. Then we evaluate the similarities in the lists of the three groups. We definitely consider not only what we want to achieve, but also what we have the ability to achieve. Both of them are important to consider. As I have learned, and Jeff Janssen has stated, ***we have to balance the "can" and the "want."*** *Once we determine the mission for the year, we do the same process for determining goals that we can set that will help us achieve our mission. We want each goal to be realistic, but also challenging for us.*

Now, once we have determined what our mission and goals will be, then we have to think about and establish what types of standards and commitments it will take to get there. It will take the involvement and investment of all of our players to be successful at our goals and mission. We will break into the three groups again and come up with ideas of different commitments. We will try to come up with around 8 or 10 as a whole in the end. We do not want to become overwhelmed, but ***we do want to be challenged****. The last thing we do is to put it all on paper so each athlete can see what they have to accomplish and what it will take to get there. We have each girl sign it and we post it up for our team to see both at practice and before games. I also will be there to help them stay focused or get refocused when needed.*

Chapter 3

Preparing for the Season

Each new season will bring its own set of challenges & surprises. Whether you are a novice or a battle-tested veteran, how well prepared you are to deal with the bumps in the road may determine the success of your season. Unless you have a crystal ball that works more clearly than mine (yeah, I bought one – willing to try anything), then there isn't any way that you can predict what might pop up during the course of a year. Some unforeseen challenges:

- Equipment Needs
- Injuries
- Moves or Move-Ins
- In-Fighting
- Scheduling Conflicts
- Transportation Issues
- Disciplinary Actions
- Accusations
- Lack of Community or Administrative Support
- Rebellious Assistants

I think you get the point; the list can virtually go on and on. So how do you handle the unthinkable or unimaginable?

Preparation

There isn't any substitute for planning ahead. Take the time prior to the season to write down as many possible issues that you might face. (I know, I know, it's going to be tough without a working crystal ball – but try!) Thoughtfully respond to each issue and record it in a planner or notebook that can be quickly referenced in a time of need.

You might think – well, that's a waste of time. Trust me, it isn't, and it will help you prepare for those bumps in the road that you don't see coming. You're never going to have all the answers, nor will you ever be able to do everything just right. However, you can give some advanced thought that is sure to help you with your problem solving and decision making.

In the event a problem rears its ugly head, try not to give a knee-jerk reaction to it. Remember you've prepared for this! Accept it without emotion, process it, and then take the time to deal with it. You'll be glad that you did!

Equipment Needs

With shrinking budgets and increasing equipment needs, you might find yourself in a less-than-desirable situation. We all know that our game requires a basic amount of equipment. Can you imagine playing the game without it? No…So how can we generate a functional amount of equipment with a limited amount of cash? Start by determining what you need v. what you want.

Program Needs

- Softballs – Game Balls & Practice Balls
- Bats
- Catching Gear
- Uniforms
- Batting Helmets (NFHS approved cages now, for high school coaches)
- Scorebooks

Okay, I know, that's a short list. And yes, I realize gloves are needed – I'm just assuming that kids have their own, which is, by the way, a dangerous assumption!

Program Wants

- Pitching Machine(s)
- Hitting Aides
- Alternative Uniforms
- Visors
- Nets & Screens
- Fungo Bats (Real Back-Saver)
- Buckets & Buckets & Buckets

- Marker Boards & Charts
- Batting Cages
- Instructional Books & Videos
- Video Equipment
- Sliding Pads & Leg Pads

The "Wants List" can go on forever, limited only by your imagination. The trick now is to balance your needs and your wants. And if your combination doesn't match up well with your administration's idea of a budget, then what is your option?

Fundraising!

This, in itself, can be a beast. Before you begin, *keep the beast leashed!* There are thousands of fundraisers, so before you begin, ask yourself the following:

- *How much money do we need to generate?*
- *How much time am I willing to devote to this?*
- *Is there anyone that I can depend on to help with this?*
- *What do I plan to do with the money as it comes in?*
- *Will my administration support this?*

Determining just how much you need to generate goes back to how you've balanced your needs and your wants. You are the only one who is going to know the answer to this question. But you do need to realize that whatever you partake in, it will take a great deal of time to organize it and see it through. This can be a headache unless you're able to find some help with it.

In the past I have employed dependable athletes with different responsibilities concerning fundraisers; however, be careful as to what you assign them to do and never allow them to be responsible for collecting money or housing inventory. It just isn't a good idea since too many things can go wrong with that. Finding a parent who is willing to undertake a fundraiser is a wonderful idea if you know that parent isn't expecting some sort of returned favor down the road.

In Cozad, our softball parent group formed their own booster club. They elected officers and helped organize everything from setting up for events to creating a bank account to handle the incoming and outgoing funds. School administrators will vary with their opinion concerning this activity, so be sure to ask before you allow a booster club such as the aforementioned to form. Remember, always ***leash the beast!***

I am a bit of a fundraising advocate. Nobody really enjoys doing it, and that's a given. However, the benefits to your program can be enormous. I'm big on having the kids feeling privileged. It gives them a sense of pride to be able to sport great apparel and prepare with excellent equipment. This fabricated sense of pride can be powerful. I relate it to how most people feel when they put on a new shirt or dress up for a special occasion. One can't help but feel a rise in confidence! It's the same for your athletes – if they feel good about themselves – they'll be more confident and will perform at a high level.

As I mentioned before, there are so many fundraisers to choose from. What's the best? Well, I'm glad you've asked. I've questioned coaches from around the country what they've found success with, so here are some ideas to get you started.

Ideas Regarding Fundraising

Amy Hayes, Portland State University / NCAA DI – Portland, OR

We run a raffle every year. Each athlete and coach gets a prize donated (so we'll have anywhere from 15 to 25 prizes - one being a big grand prize - usually a trip) and then everyone, coaches and players are expected to sell a certain amount. We usually raise anywhere from $2000 - $8000.

Ed Lantzer, Lake H.S. – Uniontown, OH

Parent volunteers and local business connections are keys to any success we have in fundraising. Also, a well-run camp or clinic can be a good way to develop good public relations within the community and still raise some money at the same time.

Terry Graver, Elkhorn H.S. – Elkhorn, NE

I have tried them all. We have one every two years – magazines, work concessions at volleyball and basketball games. The extra money is nice if you need something during the year.

Dave Johnson, Rancho Cotate H.S. – Rohnert Park, CA

We do one fundraiser before the season starts. The girls each get ten discount cards and are expected to sell them all. The card consists of discounts towards restaurants, ice cream shops etc. This fundraiser usually raises approx. $3000.00

Keith Hauber, Lake Central H.S. – St. John, IN

Our school print shop will print our schedule board from which we sell ads. It's all profit for our program.

Glenn Moore, Baylor University – Waco, TX

We raise $5,000 to $7,000 a year with a pledge per run fund drive. Each athlete is required to get $2.00 per run and pledges will not be billed for more than 200 runs. For example a .10 pledge 200 runs = a $20.00 donation. After the season we total the runs scored and bill donors for the appropriate amount. We will also list the option of paying the total amount when runs scored exceed 200; many will pay the larger amount.

Heinz Mueller, Phoenix College / NJCAA – Phoenix, AZ

Work like crazy! Any idea is worth it if you have a total team concept towards making it happen!

Tryouts

The last two seasons I've averaged about 35-40 kids who all want to be a part of our varsity team. I go into the process without having a set number that handcuffs my decision-making, but I'm generally looking for 14-16 spots. I always take an even number because it makes warming up and partner drills work smoother throughout the season.

It's imperative that you develop a *tryout form* that provides you with documentation of your evaluation process. Prior to the tryout make sure your assistants understand the form and how you plan to score or evaluate each of your players. You'll find it difficult to fairly judge so many kids with one set of eyes and it immediately involves your assistants in the decision-making process. This is important to building the trust that you will need between you and your assistant coaches. It also provides security for you if you are questioned about the evaluation process by a parent. Having your assistants' opinions and not just your own will prove that there is truly power in numbers!

So, what are you looking for in a team member?

Picking out your best players is never really too challenging. It's the last three or four spots that tend to be the most difficult to fill. That's why it's important to know exactly what you are looking for. When choosing a team, you should consider how a marginal player might contribute. Ask yourself what's important to your team. Maybe you are more concerned about team chemistry, so you take a kid who will contribute in intangible ways. Or perhaps you need someone who can serve a special skill such as a pinch runner, so you choose someone who fills a specific need. Every team is different, and each team has its own set of needs; it's up to you to fill them as you see fit.

Developing Positive Coach / Parent Relationships

As coaches, one thing that we have to remember is that we are involved in a partnership with players and parents. We have to honor that relationship and develop it in a positive way that allows for honest communication and respect. Having a good parent group will make your life much easier, and you can create that by being upfront and straightforward with them. All parents want their kids to play, all the time, and we have to respectfully dispel the notion of that happening.

If you run a program, such as a varsity program, that is designed to win rather than making sure everybody gets a chance to play, then inform your parent group of that. My history regarding how to deal with parents is to simply keep them informed. Nobody likes to be blindsided or deceived. Therefore, it's imperative that you tell not only your players but also their parents how your program operates.

We do this initially with a *pre-season parent letter*. It's a good way to introduce yourself, your philosophy, and your excitement for the upcoming season. In this letter we make sure to inform the parents about our different levels of participation and how each operates. For example, our junior varsity program focuses more on getting everyone involved because it's a developmental league; however, our varsity team is designed to produce victories.

In addition to the letter, we host a parent meeting. At the meeting we introduce all of the coaches and offer thanks to the parent group for allowing us to work with their daughters. It's at this time that we discuss how the varsity team will be chosen. We also discuss some of our rules and then answer any questions that they have. This is a tremendous opportunity to show parents that we care about what we're doing, that we're organized, and that we're serious about doing things the right way.

We make it known that we have an "open-door" policy and that we will discuss anything concerning their daughter except for playing time. We can talk about what she needs to do to be a better player, but we won't talk about why she isn't playing and someone else is. If that situation occurs, our conversation is over and if they wish to talk about it more, then they will have to arrange a meeting with the athletic director.

Our practices are open to parents. We have nothing to hide, and we encourage moms and dads to come out and see how hard we work. This makes parents feel more involved rather than creating a division between them and yourself. Remember, it's a partnership and it has to be cultivated. We have even allowed parents to help shag balls after practice if someone stays for extra reps. Just look for ways to get them involved, but maintain a level of respect and understanding.

If you can create a positive environment that involves your coaches, players and their parents, then you'll have a family atmosphere. You'll have tremendous support for your decisions and any naysayer will be quickly silenced. There is truly something special about having everyone intimately involved in what you're doing.

Additional Ideas Regarding Parent / Coach Relations

Heinz Mueller, Phoenix College / NJCAA – Phoenix, AZ

I have a barbeque and a parent meeting at the beginning of the fall season and review what the staff and team expect out of the parents for the season.

Tom Spencer, Notre Dame College – South Euclid, Ohio

Bottom line – Be HONEST with the parents. If their daughter is not good enough, then tell them; don't sugarcoat it. In addition, tell them what they will need to work on to get better.

Scott Howard, Liberty H.S. – Liberty, MO

About the only thing we as coaches can do is to be open and honest with the parents. Our school district has implemented a parent information night at the start of each sport season. This gives the coaches a chance to talk to the parents about the programs, expectations, cutting policies. I will then hold another meeting once the cuts have been made for parents and players in the program. We will discuss things more in depth at this meeting. I also have created a player handbook and parent/player contract that we will sign, saying we agree to follow the policies, including our "Chain of Command," which is a district policy about the flow of communication. I try to include the parents whenever it is appropriate, but they know that I will not discuss anything in terms of playing time, positions, and game decisions. All in all, the parents and I have a good, open relationship, and I am able to rely on them to get a lot of things done.

Ed Lantzer, Lake H.S. – Uniontown, OH

Communication! *If your players are happy, your parents are usually happy. Always communicate to your players what their expected role* *on the team is before the season starts. Make sure the player agrees to that role and have them talk it over with their parents. Usually, if a player is okay with her role and her playing time and she's having fun being a part of the team, the parents will be supportive. Also, we like to have each of our parents host at least one team dinner throughout the season. This is a great way to develop team chemistry, and it's also a nice time for parents and coaches to get to know one another away from the ball field.*

Terry Graver, Elkhorn H.S. – Elkhorn, NE

I have a pre-season parent meeting and give them player and parent expectations. This has really helped prevent many problems from even starting. I tell the parents that playing time is not something we discuss. I want the player to discuss all issues with the coaching staff.

Amy Hayes, Portland State University / NCAA DI – Portland, OR

At the beginning of each year we have a team dinner where parents, friends and other family members are involved. We want it to be a family, and we want them to know that their children are important to us, but I encourage the athletes to speak for themselves if issues come up, rather than their parents. They need to learn to communicate and problem solve on their own two feet. We also keep our parents up to date with our newsletters, travel itineraries, and community service opportunities, etc.

Chapter 4

Practice Planning

I spend a tremendous amount of time preparing for each practice. And this madness begins well before the season starts. Prior to the season I create a *practice checklist*. This checklist is a general template that I modify each season, depending on our team's forecast needs. Sitting down with a calendar, I plot the number of available days we have to practice and set weekly practice goals. There are aspects of the game we want to teach everyday. Then there are elements that we want to add as the season progresses. If you throw it all at them at once, chances are they aren't going to be very good at it, unless they've already been doing it for a long time.

Within each practice we want to impress fundamentals. The basic concepts of hitting, fielding, and throwing are emphasized daily. We try to do this in a variety of ways so that our instruction doesn't become stagnant. In the drill sections of this book you'll be able to find many different drills that virtually seek to accomplish the same fundamental repetition.

Each week, we want to implement a new strategic concept. For example, we may want to spend a portion of a practice one week on talking about rundowns. Then in week two we will develop a quick reminder drill to reemphasize the previous week's learning, while we move on to a different strategic concept. This pattern is followed through the season so, because of advanced planning, by the end of our season we will have implemented all of the items we deemed to be important.

Our practices average about two hours in length. This is a good number because it's long enough to get everything accomplished, yet it isn't so long that it dissuades individuals from sticking around afterwards and getting extra help. Practices tend to be longer the first few weeks of the season and decrease in time as the season progresses.

We stress fundamentals every single day. During the first few weeks of the year, prior to our first contest, our practices are fully dedicated to repeating the fundamentals of the game in as many different drills as we can conceive. As the season wears on, based on our season practice plan, we will start implementing strategic ideas and start reducing the amount of time we dedicate to fundamentals.

It's essential that you set the pace for your practice and be consistent. Develop an attitude about how you approach practice, and expect your players to reflect that. Our practice time is valuable, and our coaching staff stresses that to our players. We want our practices to be fun, but we have to maintain maximum effort throughout the duration of our time. We want a fast-moving practice with very little down time. Our players know from day one what we expect from them within each practice. As your program grows, returning players will set this example for you and bring others up to their level of effort.

Practice Guidelines

- Quick Transitions Between Drills
- Constant Chatter / Communication
- Do It 'til It's Perfect
- "Can't" Won't Work
- When In Doubt – Hustle

Four years ago, a Division I coach stopped by one of our practices to watch one of our players in a practice setting. After the practice he confessed that our practice was one of the best he had ever witnessed.

This was the ultimate compliment. But while it was a good practice, it was a normal practice. We were well into our season by that point, and our players were well-versed in all of our drill work, but it was our enthusiasm and how we quickly transitioned into each drill that really impressed this particular coach.

The amount of time many teams waste between drills is astonishing. How much time does it take your team to prepare for the next drill? Do they walk? Do they need a drink break in between each drill? Do they stand around and talk? Do you and your assistants stand around and talk? Is the equipment set up and ready to go?

Every practice we generate will be broken down minute by minute for the time we have allotted. I use a watch and seldom will I ever venture too far off schedule. If our team doesn't get a concept after 15 minutes, which is the maximum for any drill, then we need to leave it and revisit the idea another day. Your players will get just as frustrated as you, which will likely be counterproductive. The advantage of keeping a disciplined schedule will result in a fast-moving, goal-oriented, and focused practice.

Prepare yourself in advance, and plan how your team will transition between each drill. Build in drink breaks that do no more than serve their purpose - **it's a drink break!** Drink breaks can turn into gossip sessions, and if allowed, kids will display the laziest body language ever seen to mankind. Don't allow it; give them an opportunity to get a drink, cool off if necessary, and then get them focused again. If we need an extended drink break because of the heat or exhaustion, I use that time to talk to the team. I might tell a motivational story, or it may be something as simple as instructions as to what uniform we'll be wearing for the next contest. Players do not need unsupervised time at your practices to gossip; otherwise, it may poison your team chemistry.

Our practices typically follow a routine that allows our team leaders to get practice started everyday. This gives your team a sense of empowerment and teaches them to be self starters. Our team captains begin practice promptly by taking the team for a jog around the field followed by a detailed stretching routine. As coaches we stand aside and discuss the practice plan for the day. We ask that our warm-up be focused but lively. We encourage a lot of softball-related talk and enthusiasm. After jogging and stretching, players begin our *throwing routine* with their partner.

Early in the season we will do a set number of quick-hitting fundamental drills designed to give maximum repetition for fielding balls in a variety of ways. These drills are partner drills as well and after the first couple of days it requires little instruction to get them going. The jog, stretch, warm-up and any quick-hitting fundamental drills will take 45 minutes of our practice. Take a look at an example of one of our practice plans that is broken down into different segments.

Dissecting the Practice Plan

Practice Plan Example:

BW Softball - "Being our best everyday in everyway!"

9/15/05

Quote of the Day: *When you drink the water, remember the spring.*
~ Chinese Proverb

Weekly Concept : Infielders – Rundowns
Outfielders – Gap Communication

Daily Concept : Fundamental Defensive Improvement
Balance in the Box

Reminders: Bus Departure @ 3:45
White Uniforms
Team Dinner Saturday at Amanda's / Noon

3:35 – 3:55 Jog, Stretch

3:55 – 4:10 Throwing

4:10 – 4:13 Short Hop Drill

4:13 – 4:16 Partner Ground Balls (Lateral)

4:16 – 4:19 Short / Long Drill

4:19 – 4:20 Drink Break - *Give Team Reminders!*

This is a typical script that would be used for almost every practice of the year. We rotate our *daily quick-hitters*; these drills are primarily defense-oriented. Even though you are essentially using the same routine every day, you will keep your team motivated by changing these quick-hitters daily.

We typically start dividing our team into a positional breakdown segment at this point in practice. If your practice is disciplined and you've set forth high expectations for conduct, you can do this without having an army of coaches. I've had as few as one assistant to as many as four assistants to help facilitate breakdown drills. Regardless, have your breakdown drills designed in a manner that you can efficiently use the area you're provided with. Take a look at what I mean:

Corner Infielders

Area: 1st Base Foul Territory

Drills: Dig Drill, Reaction Drill, Backhand Drill

Time: 10 minutes

Middle Infielders

Area: Middle of the Infield around 2nd Base

Drills: Laterals, Tosses, Footwork on the Bag

Time: 10 minutes

Pitchers / Catchers

Area: 3rd Base Foul Territory

Drills: Pitcher Warm-up, Pitch Simulation

Time: 40 minutes

Outfielders

Area: Centerfield

Drills: Drop-step Drills, Crow Hop Drills, Gap Communication Drills, Outfield Football

Time: 20 minutes

A big part of our game is about specialized skills. Therefore, it's important that a segment of your practice reflects that. Our breakdown drills allow us to spend anywhere from 10 -20 minutes every day on these specialized skills with a good deal of repetition for each. Continuing our *practice plan*:

4:20 – 4:40 Breakdown Drills for Infielders / Outfielders

4:20 – 4:30 Corners - Dig, Reaction, Backhand

Middle - Laterals, Tosses, Footwork

OF - Drop-steps, Crow-hops, Gaps

4:30 – 4:40 IF - Infield Cycles

OF – Outfield Football

4:20 – 5:00 Pitchers / Catchers - Warm-up, Pitch Simulation

4:40 – 4:50 Team Merry-Go-Round Drill (excluding p/c)

We manage the extra time when we don't have our pitchers / catchers by implementing team-oriented drills.

4:50 – 5:00 Partner Tee-Work for INF / OF

5:00 – 5:10 Hitting Progression Drills (Full Squad)

5:10 – 5:35 Live Hitting

5:35 – 5:40 Conditioning: Base Cycles

5:40 – 5:45 Cool Down / Closing Comments

It's important when you plan your practices that you focus on fundamental skills. You may be a defensive-minded coach, or you may have a team the needs to focus more on offense. In 2001, we allowed 17 runs in the 28 games we played during the season. 75% of our focus in practice was on defense. Going into the season we felt that we would be good enough offensively, but we really had to focus on catching and throwing the ball. It paid off; we were able to win the state championship that season behind great pitching and defense - but only because going into the season we understood our needs. We then focused on those needs and ultimately found success. Conversely, during this last season, we hit every single day, and focused 75% of our team on offensive drills and situations. We had a lot of returnees on defense who caught the ball well, but most couldn't hit water if they fell out of a boat. As a result of our preparation, our team hit more than .125 points higher and set numerous school records for offense and wins. The point is, know your team and then design your practices based on your team's needs.

Chapter 5

Game-Planning

We've always operated primarily under the idea that we should worry more about what we're going to do rather than what our opponent might do. That isn't to say that we don't do a tremendous amount of advanced planning with scouting reports and game charts. However, we tend not to provide our team with too much information regarding any opponent. Instead, we usually develop a list of things we have to accomplish to be successful within any given contest. From that list, generated with the help of my assistants, we pick two or three key elements to share with the team.

Developing Keys to Victory

(ex.) Keys – McCook 9/15

1. Execute all bunt situations

2. Be aware of all runners at all times

3. Hit it the other way.

Our coaching staff understood that, in order to beat a well-coached and gifted McCook team, we had to be able to execute all bunt opportunities. Knowing that the game would likely be close, the team that best took advantage of this aspect of the game might gain an edge. Second, we knew that McCook was an aggressive team that would steal and take extra bases when given the opportunity. Therefore, we wanted to stress the importance of paying attention to base runners. Last, our scouting indicated that McCook pitchers lived on the outer half of the plate. So, we emphasized to our team to look to hit it the other way.

Now as coaches, we knew a lot more about McCook. We knew that their leadoff hitter would slap on the first two pitches and then she'd switch to the other side. We knew that the two-hole hitter would never swing at a first pitch, and I could go on and on about their hitter tendencies. Also, we had knowledge as to what they did in 1st & 3rd situations on both offense and defense; we knew what their pitcher's "out-pitch" was, we knew about their delayed stealing, their centerfielder had a cannon, their left-fielder couldn't run, their third baseman could be bunted on, etc.

The point is, if we've scouted, we will always know more than our team will know about the opposition. The real genius is in sharing what needs to be shared so that your team can benefit from your advanced planning. To tell them everything you know will be counterproductive, because they'll focus on too many things and never be able to perform well with any of them. Just like the old adage "a jack of all trades, a master of none." We don't want that for our team, but instead focus them in on a few key aspects and then prepare them to succeed.

Scouting

Essential to game-planning is scouting. Although when you scout, what the heck are you looking for?

Through the years I've been fortunate enough to make several friends through competitions and clinics. This network of friends has provided me with a reliable source of information about teams that we play. I use our state activity association's website to find everyone's schedule. Then I cross-reference my schedule with that of our opposition and learn who I need to email and when. From that I may send out three or four friendly scouting requests. That doesn't mean that I abandon the idea of seeing a team firsthand, but it can be challenging to do so when some game times start before your own practice ends, or when extended travel is involved.

Understand that this network that you establish will also expect information from you. My philosophy on this is to give every coach who requests a scouting report a response immediately. Sometimes it may be as simple as just acknowledging that I received their request, and then I inform them of when they can expect to receive my report. I do this because I think that it is common courtesy, and it lets the coach know that his request is important to me. After all, when I request information it's important to me.

Tip: *There are other ways to scout that don't involve leaving practice early or spending your day off in the bleachers. Using your computer and contacting other coaches through email can be just as informative.*

Scouting Pitchers

When scouting any team, we start with the pitcher. More than any other thing, we want to know what she does and how she does it. We have a checklist of items that we look for when scouting a pitcher. First of all, we want to know what her tendencies are regarding counts. What pitch does she throw on a 0-1 count? How about 0-2 or 2-0? Knowing can be valuable when issuing signs to your hitters or when determining what play you might employ late in a game.

In the 2003 state tournament, we drew a tough 1st round opponent. They had a pitcher who currently holds almost every pitching record in our state's record book. Their record was 30-1, with the only loss coming in a one-run game. She dominated as a hard thrower with a plethora of other pitches. We scouted her twice, and in both contests I noticed that almost every first pitch was a strike, right down the middle. Now, it was coming in consistently at 63-64 mph, but it was straight as an arrow. For a week, our batting practice consisted of having our pitching machine hurling the ball at its top speed. Each day we moved the machine closer to the hitter, in an attempt to prepare our team for what they'd see. By the end of the week we were having moderate success hitting off the machine, because we knew where the pitch would be and we knew we were supposed to be swinging.

We took that same approach into the game. We wanted to swing at every first pitch. In the first three innings we put up five runs. Overall, we struck out 17 times in the game, but we won 5-1. I attribute the win to two things. One, we prepared our team for the speed that they'd be seeing. Second, we were able to discover this particular pitcher's tendency of throwing a first pitch strike. Thus, we were able to jump out to the lead before eventually they caught on to what we were doing.

Without having scouted this team, we would have never been able to appropriately prepare for the game. Sure, through word-of-mouth we could have prepared for the speed in the same way. However, without knowing that we should swing at the first pitch, then we likely would not have been able to string together any number of hits.

What's Her Best Pitch?

Determining a pitcher's best pitch is often more important than how hard she throws. Speed is a funny thing. Pitchers who throw more slowly than others have traditionally been more difficult for our teams to hit. It's all a timing thing, and hitters can generally adjust to speed, usually better up than down. What can really benefit you or your team is having knowledge as to what pitch the pitcher turns to when she really needs to make a pitch. Maybe it's what she likes to throw to get the strikeout. Maybe it's the pitch she wants to make to get ahead in the count. Or it could be what she throws when she's in desperate need of throwing a strike.

Think about your own pitchers. What is their favorite pitch? If you call the pitches, you should know what pitch you need to call when you really need a good one. Every pitcher has a favorite pitch. When you're scouting, find out what that pitch is, and then use that information to your advantage.

Is she Emotionally Stable?

Now I don't intend to inflict any emotional pain and suffering upon any child, and that's not what this is about. It's about examining a pitcher's emotional demeanor and looking for strategies to shake her in the circle. Is she distracted easily? How does she handle pressure? Does she have a deliberate pace? Does she interact with her teammates? What is her attitude like?

We want our pitchers to find a level of nirvana when they are pitching – at a perfect, relaxed pace; we want our pitchers to be in control. Conversely then, we have to assume that we want the opposite for the competition. Therefore, we look for ways to control the pace on offense, to be distracting without being annoying, and to give the pitcher the idea that we, the offense, are in fact in control. Our hitters subconsciously do this every time they dig into the batter's box. Our hitters are instructed to raise their back hand to the umpire, pausing for time, and leave it up until they are ready to hit. The umpire will not award time until the hitter is ready. We can also ask for time and step out, and we might also have an offensive conference between coach and hitter. There are many things that can be done to offensively control the pace and establish control.

We want our dugout loud and supportive. Not necessarily to distract the pitcher, but if it is distracting, then obviously, that's an advantage. We look for every possible edge to establish ourselves as the dominant team. If the opposition makes a few mistakes, we may drop a bunt and try to further frustrate them and, most likely, their pitcher. There are many things you can do, many of which you can probably think of that we haven't. Some of these strategies will work against some pitchers, and then some won't work at all. Most importantly, just prepare your team in advance, scout the opposition, and then employ what you think will work.

Scouting the Offense

Aside from developing a detailed report on what a pitcher does, we want to also know if there are any glaring weaknesses that their hitters possess. This information is strictly for our coaching staff to use to better call pitches. We examine stances, swing paths, hand posit... swing tendencies, and flaws in the stride.

Stances

Open Stance (front foot farther away from the plate) – *Pitch Outside*

Closed Stance (front foot closer to the plate) – *Pitch Inside*

Hunched Stance – *Pitch Up in the Zone*

Tall Stance – *Pitch Down in the Zone*

Shifting, Unbalanced Stance – *Use Off-Speed pitches*

Swing Paths

Downward Path – *Pitch Down in the Zone*

Upward Path – *Pitch Up in the Zone*

Long Swing (Throwing Hands Out) – *Hard Pitches in on the Hands*

Short Swing (Keeping Hands In) – *Breaking Pitches Away*

Inside-Out Swing – *Hard Pitches in on the Hands*

Dead-Pull – *Hard Pitches Away*

Hand Positioning

Hands High – *Pitch Down and In*

Hands Low – *Pitch Up and Away*

Hands Moving Forward – *Use Off-Speed Pitches*

Hands Too Far Back – *Hard Pitches in on the Hands*

Stride Flaws

Steps Out During Stride – *Pitch Away*

Steps toward the Plate – *Pitch Inside*

Shifts Weight Forward – *Use Off-Speed Pitches*

Keeps Weight on the Backside – *Pitch Up and Inside*

Back Knee Falls upon Stride – *Pitch Up*

Stands Up When Striding – *Pitch Down*

Finding an Edge

When planning to scout, understand your own team and what your team does well. Where might you have an edge? Where do you need to gain an edge? How can your team benefit from your scouting a particular team? You will match up differently with the various teams that you'll face on your schedule. Having a firm understanding of your own team by discovering their strengths and weaknesses will help you prepare and scout your opposition. Also, sometimes it isn't as important to scout the players as it is the coach and his or her tendencies. Below you will find a series of questions that may reveal an edge while scouting.

Questions to Answer While Scouting:

- What count do they steal on?

- Do they conventionally use the sacrifice bunt?
- Do they take pitches? If so, when?
- Will they bunt for hits?
- What do they do in a 1st & 3rd situation? (Offensively & Defensively)
- What situations dictate moving their outfield?
- Do outfielders shift according to pitch selection?
- Which player comfortably fields bunts?
- Will the catcher throw behind runners who aggressively take leads?
- Are they alert to possible squeeze plays?
- Do they attempt to get lead outs first?
- How do they cover on bunts? (Is their leftfielder slow?)
- Do runners aggressively round bases?
- Who is their worst fielder?
- Which player has the worst arm?
- What player(s) crack under pressure?
- Do outfielders aggressively field ground balls?
- Which players in their lineup will they sacrifice bunt with?

- How does the team play when trailing after 4 innings?
- How does the team play when leading after 4 innings?

After collecting this information, it's a good idea to file it away somewhere so that you can quickly retrieve it if needed. We use three-ring folders and simply shelve scouting reports by season. With each new season, we then have a quick reference to help us with our game-planning. I understand coaches and personnel change from year to year; however, it does provide you with something so that you don't go into a contest blindly.

The important thing to scouting and keeping a record of reports is that you are able to aptly use the information. You likely won't be able to implement everything you know about a given team, nor should you try. Instead find two or three nuggets of information that can help you with your decision making and possibly give you an edge.

Tip: Coach Natalie Poole on Scouting

There are many things that I look for when scouting an opponent. I believe that the information gathered can be useful in preparing for competition. I always look at both offense and defense.

When scouting their offense, I identify the players in their lineup, both their name and jersey number. I also write down whether they hit left-handed, right-handed, or if they are a left-handed slapper. I try to identify their tendencies at the plate (ex., if they are first pitch swingers, if they chase pitches out of the strike zone, how they hit pitches inside or outside, up or down, and the changeup). I identify if they foul any pitches off hard, if they surprise (drag) bunt, and if they usually see lots of pitches in their at bats. I also pay attention to the batter's speed on the bases.

Along with watching individual batters, I also pay attention to the offensive strategy of the coach. Does the coach like to sacrifice bunt, slap, or hit and run? Do they squeeze bunt when runners are at third base with less than two outs? Is the coach aggressive on the bases? What do the hitters do in first and third situations?

I also watch their mental game. Are the hitters easily intimidated, do they check swing a lot (second guessing), or do they get frustrated easily with the calls from the umpire?

We also scout their pitchers. We keep track of the name and number of the pitchers, and also their tendencies. We list what types of pitches they throw, what the pitcher likes to throw early in the count and late in the count. What is her go-to pitch and what does she throw when behind in the count? Does she use a changeup, when, and is it effective? What is the pitcher's speed? Does she get rattled easily, and can her rhythm be broken easily?

I also scout the team defensively. I list who is playing and where. I list their strengths and weaknesses (arms, range, reactions to the ball). I look to see if the corners can get to the bunt and handle it effectively. I watch the outfielder's arms and depth at which they usually play. Can the catcher receive and block the ball well, is she a leader on the field, and how is her arm? I watch how they handle pressure situations and how they execute first and third defensive plays. As you can see, there is a lot to watch and take in, but all of it can aid in getting prepared to be successful against your opponent.

Chapter 6

Pitching

"Mentally, we want our pitchers and catchers to be confident, determined leaders on the field."

~ Coach Ed Lantzer, Lake H.S. – Uniontown, OH

Where will your success on the field start? In the circle! Think about her importance; she touches the ball more than any other player on the field. She's also the one everybody watches; she's the heartbeat of your team. A pitcher's demeanor, attitude, and ability to handle pressure situations can make or break your team.

Pitchers do not have to possess overpowering "Stuff" to be effective!

I've been fortunate enough to have been blessed with talented pitchers during my coaching career. However, each possessed a different mental makeup, which was ultimately the difference in how I would rank their effectiveness. Today, it seems like most of the teams we play have someone who throws at least 60 mph. In our area, this was simply uncommon five years ago. A kid who threw that hard was a dominator, and if you had one, then you were destined to win a majority of your games. Now with more hard throwers out there, hitters are being exposed to more of it and, thus, have adjusted. Simply put, the players are constantly evolving and changing.

With more and more parity amongst players and teams, it makes the mental edge evermore important. We believe this starts in the circle. Our team's identity will be formed by how our pitcher competes. We stress this idea to our pitchers from the beginning of the season. They have to know how important their role is, and we encourage them to grasp it. Some might argue that this applies more pressure to the pitcher. I disagree. The pressure is inevitable; it comes with the position, whether you talk about it or not. As mentioned before, all eyes are on the pitcher; she touches the ball more than anyone!

This huge responsibility can be a burden for the pitcher if she isn't capable of handling such pressure. My experience is that most pitchers can handle this if they've been given the necessary tools to deal with it. Knowing just what to do and say can be difficult. I suggest that you check out *jeffjanssen.com* – where you will find some great softball-related resources that focus on the mental aspect of the game. You will not only find great resources for your pitchers, but you'll also find an abundance of helpful information for your players, team, and program.

I have used many of Jeff Janssen's products, and I can tell you that his approach is proven and successful. He is also known throughout the coaching world, as well as the business sector. In regard to finding a mental edge for your pitcher, I specifically recommend, "Mental Training for Softball." In it you will find tips and ideas on visualization, self talk, goal setting, and concentration. All of these concepts can be effectively incorporated into any mental training you wish to engage in with your pitchers.

Mental Conditioning

We mentally prepare our athletes, and particularly our pitchers, throughout the year, with much of it being done in the off-season. Constantly look for articles of triumph and inspiration, cut them out and randomly give them to your athletes. From the feedback that you'll get, you will see how much they enjoy your efforts. For one this shows the athlete that you care, and second, you're feeding them positive information.

Seek out your pitcher and ask her what she thought about a particular article. Ask her what she thought made the story interesting, or what made the central figure or team successful. Start to plant the seeds for mental growth. Have your athletes think about success and allow them to discover what makes others so successful.

Visualize Success

For our pitchers, we specifically have found some success in teaching them how to visualize being successful. We do this through a series of drills that begin in our off-season program. Our goal is to have our pitchers confident and mentally prepared for all situations when they step into the circle for the first game of our season.

It can be difficult to get your pitcher to buy into what you're teaching her if she's working with another pitching coach or summer coach or even an overbearing parent! The best approach to this conflict is to communicate with everyone involved and, hopefully, they will try to implement some of your mental strategies to better improve the individual.

I do realize egos can get in the way, and unfortunately, they often do. To completely work around what seems like an unworkable situation; simply wait until a few weeks before your season starts when you will have less distraction from other voices. The important thing is the instruction itself and how consistent you can be in applying it to your pitcher's learning.

In the Moment

Our approach to achieving a successful mental approach for our pitchers revolves around what we call "Being in the Moment." And this can only be achieved through having a mind that is free from distraction. We tell our pitchers that every pitch is a new experience. We want them to embrace these experiences as opportunities to succeed.

How many times have you seen a pitcher dominate for five innings only to implode and lose her focus after a teammate makes a mistake, a parent starts coaching, or an umpire blows a call? It happens a lot. I can't quote any statistical information regarding it, but I'm confident you've seen it, too.

So, if this is a common occurrence, and if you believe as I do that the most important player on the field is in the circle, then shouldn't you spend time equipping her with the tools she needs to combat this negative action? We strongly believe in it; thus, we commit a lot of time to mentally prepare our pitchers to be calm, confident, and ultimately successful.

Breathe

When any of our players start showing signs of pressure or a lack of confidence, we remind them to focus on their breathing. Everybody has to breathe; therefore, it's an easy point of reference. When asked to focus on their breathing, players will immediately begin to relax. We ask our players to hear their breathing, while thinking of nothing else. I often refer to it as a *"mental vacation."*

Tell your pitchers to think of a place that they enjoy the most. Have them refer to that place during their *"mental vacation."* They should retreat to this place every time they receive the ball back from the catcher. We remind them that a vacation is relaxing! So we want them to take their time in making their way back into the circle. Control the pace of the game and find a comfortable rhythm. Return back into the circle and step onto the pitching plate only after they've forgotten about their previous pitch and started to "hear" their breathing. This routine should be done during warm-ups and practices, as well as competitions.

The goal is to be able to focus for several short segments of time as opposed to having your pitcher stay concentrating during the entire game. It's virtually impossible to do so, and asking her to do it will only increase the pressure that she'll already be battling. Try staring at any random object for an extended period of time. How long does it take before the object becomes blurry? How long does it take before your mind begins to wander? If you're like most of us, it doesn't take longer for either, and if you're aging as I am, the former happens prior to the latter! If we can admit that concentrating on anything for an extended period of time can be difficult, then why would we ask our pitcher to do it?

Concentration

I've heard so many people from the dugout, as well as the stands shout out instructions for players to concentrate. I'm not saying that they're wrong, but their expectations are a little unrealistic. All players need to be taught how and when to effectively concentrate. It isn't something that just naturally happens for most people! And for the reasons already mentioned, it's even more important that your pitchers are able to do so.

Not to sound redundant, but the importance of equipping your players, especially your pitchers, with the necessary tools to handle pressure situations is vital. Being able to apply those tools in game-like situations can only be achieved through repetitive experiences. Practices can be made to simulate these situations, and coaches should be cognitive of its importance.

Pitcher's Reminders

- Take Mental Vacations (At the Appropriate Times!!!)
- Breathe
- Relax
- Focus
- Every Pitch is a New Experience

Additional Insights on Pitching

Glenn Moore, Baylor University – Waco, TX

Everyone wants a dominant pitcher but few have one. As a pitching philosophy I would like to have three different styles:

1. *A power pitcher with a good change.*
2. *A mid-speed pitcher with good movement.*
3. *If the first two were right-handed, I would like a lefty.*

I like different looks because even though all hitters do not hit alike on a team – many do and all teams will eventually figure out a pitcher. Change is good and knowing when to pull a pitcher is a gift. Sometimes I feel I have the gift and other times I've lost it. The key is to not just know your pitcher's abilities but to KNOW your pitchers. Their mental strength, endurance, competitiveness, and pain tolerance along with talent will also factor in to decision making.

Keith Hauber, Lake Central H.S. – St. John, IN

Our pitchers throw about 150-200 pitches in a normal practice: 30 fast balls; 20 fastball / changeup; 20 fastball / rise; 20 fastball / curve; then we do spot throwing (J pitching) with the same sets. In a tournament we will have our pitchers throw a simulated game for the opponent we are facing.

Amy Hayes, Portland State University / NCAA DI – Portland, OR

Even if you are 5'2"- you should always throw like you're 6'3". Stay tall and long- Full arm circle (relaxed not stiff) with good balance throughout your delivery. Be sure to use your legs and push off towards your catcher and not directly up. Once the ball is at the top of your circle, be sure to let your hips clear naturally while keeping your weight fairly balanced – a slight tip in the shoulders, but for the most part, shoulders over hips over knees. Toe touch and finish pitch with a relaxed but strong arm. Arm speed = velocity, wrist = movement and leg drive = power and stability.

Ed Lantzer, Lake H.S. – Uniontown, OH

At Lake, we've been pretty fortunate to have solid pitching. We rely on our pitchers to put in the extra practice with their pitching coaches year-round. During the season, it's important that our pitchers are physically fit and mentally tough. Stamina and leg strength are key to a productive and injury-free season. Mentally, we want our pitchers and catchers to be confident, determined leaders on the field. Together, they have to be able to control a ballgame defensively. If you have a coach who calls pitches, the three of them must be on the same page with a common game plan on attacking hitters.

Scott Howard, Liberty H.S. – Liberty, MO

It is important that the pitchers be involved in fielding practice. Why do so many of us "panic" when a routine ball is hit to our pitcher? We don't know if she'll field it cleanly and then we worry about where that short throw may end up. Ask yourself this question, when a ball is hit to your pitcher and she's ready to throw to first, what do you find yourself saying? I bet many coaches are saying, "Step and throw!" It's important to give pitchers many reps on fielding and throwing. There should be no reason why your pitchers aren't making the same routine plays as the other fielders; after all, it is a position that needs to be fielded.

Special Insert, by George Jones, Professional Pitching Instructor

"So You Want Your Daughter To Be A Pitcher?"

The development of any young athlete is a Long Slow Process. This is because it takes time to learn the skills and athletes change significantly in both their physical as well as their mental approach to the game. As the skills become more complex, the longer it takes to refine and evolve them.

Out of every 100 eight-year old "Wanna-Be Pitchers," there may be approximately 10-12 of them still doing their thing by the time they reach 17 years of age. Those remaining few will most likely be Select Pitchers seeking College Scholarships. Where did they all go?

Some disappear around age 15-16 as Jobs, Boys & Cars get in the way, but for most of them, they left because they got pushed too far, too fast(burn out). At young ages they were put into roles that were beyond their physical and mental capabilities. Eventually they failed on the field and they quit pitching. Being responsible for carrying a team, winning every game and pitching four- plus games per weekend is fine for a Collegiate Pitcher but is not appropriate for an eleven-year old pitcher!

The pitchers that survive the long haul tend to out-work everyone else. Behind them are the parents (mostly Dad) who make them practice when they don't want to and has higher expectations than everybody else! Parents tend to fall into two categories:

A. *Those that push forward blindly, always adding and changing but never allowing enough time for development. These situations always fail!*

B. *Those that have savvy and insight and allow their daughters to grow and evolve along with their pitching game. They may push a little and have high expectations but they temper it with "Common Sense," knowing that sometimes a rest is a good thing. These situations usually survive the ups and downs of the seasons.*

Key Word: **Common Sense**

Yours in sports,

George

George W. Jones
Professional Instructor

Chapter 7

The Catcher – Your Pitcher's Best Friend

"I think the catcher's position often gets overlooked. A lot of times they get stuck shagging for the coach and don't get a lot of drill time. The skills of a catcher do require some technique training."

~ Janice Esses, Bethany College - Lindsborg, KS

In order for a pitcher to reach her potential she must have a serviceable, if not good, catcher to throw to. The pitcher will really rely on the catcher for a good target, a consistent pace, and emotional support. A good catcher will value the importance of this relationship and work hard to excel in these areas. Behind the pitcher, the catcher is the second most important position on the field.

Catchers rarely get the accolades, respect, and recognition that they deserve. Perhaps it's because they hide behind a mask; I don't know the real reasons why. I'm digressing, but the point is, catchers are vitally important to your pitchers and the success of your team. I've already used the idea that pitchers touch the ball more than any other player; therefore, they are automatically the most important, so using that same philosophy, it's easy to anoint the catcher as the second most important player on the field.

We teach our catchers their responsibilities as soon as possible. For many of the catchers I have coached, this has come during our off-season workouts. Catchers learn very early during pitching lessons that they are not just there to receive pitches. We emphasize the importance of setting-up properly, giving a good target, and then quickly getting the ball back to the pitcher.

Setting Up

We divide the plate into three zones. Zone 1 is the left outer edge of the plate as the catcher sees it. Zone 2 is the middle of the plate, where we rarely throw. Zone 3 is the right outer edge of the plate, where we throw most of our right-handed hitting opponents. The catcher is taught to straddle each of those zones depending on the situation, the pitch, and the desired outcome. The middle of her body should be centered over the selected zone prior to giving the pitcher her sign.

We want our pitchers not to worry about location, but instead to keep a clear mind and simply throw the requested pitch to the target. We require that our catcher do all the thinking in conjunction with the coaches. I have made a habit of calling each pitch; however, whether you do that or not, there is still a benefit to properly instructing your catchers how to set up to receive a pitch.

Good Targets

It is essentially important that the pitcher sees a consistent target. In our philosophy we want to keep things as simple as possible for the pitcher; this requires her to be comfortable as well. Nothing can be more distracting than a catcher who cannot consistently show a good target. Control the things you can control; giving a consistent target is one thing that every catcher can control.

We achieve this by asking our catcher to always center the glove in the middle of her body. This will always give a pitcher a frame of reference. We will on occasion use a slightly lower or slightly higher target, but we never show a target left or right of center. We feel that by being able to provide this consistent target, we're then able to tell the pitcher to simply throw to the mitt. And, to our pitcher's advantage, she is able to see that target in a consistent manner in reference to the catcher's body.

Return to Sender

We ask our pitchers to do a lot in terms of their mental routines. Therefore, it's imperative that the catcher do her part to keep that routine as consistent as possible. Thus, we want our catchers to quickly return the ball to the pitcher so that she can start enjoying her "mental vacation." As you notice, I've been feeding you a lot in terms of consistency and routine. With that in mind, it's important for us to make sure that our catchers understand the importance of this process.

The catcher should focus on making good throws back to the pitcher. There really shouldn't be any difference in how she does this. Obviously, with runners on base and a need to check runners, the catcher has to be mindful. Otherwise, there isn't any reason why there isn't a continual effort to keep the pitcher in her comfort zone.

Signs

Traditionally, I have always signaled signs to our catcher to be relayed to our pitcher. I know that every coach has an opinion on this subject. For me, I like to eliminate a lot of the thinking for my pitcher and catcher, so that they can find a level of comfort within the game. This doesn't mean that my pitchers and catchers aren't able to predict what I'm going to call, because most of them can. By the midpoint of every season, my catchers are quick to tell me that they knew what pitches I was going to call. This reassures me that they are able to think about the game, as I want them to do, without the responsibility of having to make decisions on which pitch to throw.

We ask our catchers to get two signs. The first sign they receive from the dugout is *location*. The second sign they will receive is the *pitch* we've selected to throw. The only sign they relay to the pitcher is the pitch. We instruct our catchers to immediately move to the location upon receiving the sign and then relay the pitch selected onto the pitcher. Thus, the pitcher sees one sign, and all she has to do is simply throw the pitch selected to the catcher's target. We've found this system to be very effective and simple enough for our pitchers to remain relaxed.

There are some obvious disadvantages to setting up your location early. For one, you risk the chance of a batter taking a peek back, or an astute coach screaming down the line to look for a certain location. We think these disadvantages are outweighed by the consistency that setting up early provides for our routine. Furthermore, umpires are able to get a long look at where your catcher is setting up, and we feel that we get more strikes called on borderline pitches because of this. Also, isn't hitting about reacting more than thinking? So is it really that advantageous for a hitter to hear teammates, coaches, or fans screaming out a location?

Tip: Keep it Tucked

When relaying a sign we want our catchers to keep the sign tucked. Any sign that is given too far forward or too low will give the opposition an opportunity to pick the sign. The sign should be given high in the crotch with the knees pointing forward to protect the signal being given. If you think your signs have been compromised, then have a backup plan in place. We simply move each number forward one spot, so then a one is essentially a two and so on.

Chapter 8

Infielders

"So much of our game happens in the infield, so I spend a lot of time with the infielders. Nearly every practice devotes time to fundamentals. The goal is to get the players to be solid in their fielding abilities."

~ Scott Howard, Liberty H.S. – Liberty, MO

There isn't a good way to describe infield responsibilities without individually breaking down each position. Every position has its own set of requirements, and players must possess certain characteristics to completely fulfill the demands of each. Through daily breakdown drills we try to replicate the techniques needed to be successful with each position. Eventually we bring it all back together with our team infield drills. The goal is to have individual parts working cohesively to maximize our productivity.

Fielding Techniques

Fielding Straight On

We initially teach all of our infield prospects to essentially field the ball exactly the same. It's almost robotic in how we want them to properly field a ground ball. We ask that all of our players, regardless of position, take a right foot, left foot approach to the ball. (Unless they are left-handed, then it's just opposite) We want them to field the ball in front of them, left of middle, glove hand fingers pointing downward, with the throwing hand on top with the fingers pointing upward. And what we tell them is that we want to see the top of their head, if they have a pony-tail we want it to "pop!" Seeing the top of their head means that their nose is down, and, hopefully, they are then tracking the ball with their eyes. Upon receiving the ball, we want the fielder to "funnel" the ball to the belly button. We require that they overemphasize this action to stress its importance. The reason for the "funneling" action is to try to promote soft hands.

Fielding to the Glove Hand Side

We then will offer balls to the glove hand side of the fielder. We teach a crossover move. The crossover is the quickest possible move requiring the least amount of movement to field a ball that is hit to either side. Always, we want the crossover done without making a jab-step prior to doing it. Watch your players when you do any crossover drill and make sure that they are practicing good habits by pivoting rather than jab-stepping before crossing over. Once our fielder has made a good crossover move, then she should attempt to position herself to field the ball as she would with a ball hit straight at her. The only difference that we have is that we've now had to move laterally to position ourselves to perform the same fundamental technique.

Fielding to the Throwing Hand Side

We don't often want our middle infielders making a backhanded play unless it's absolutely necessary. Anytime a fielder can get in front of a ball, it automatically increases her chances of making a quicker play on the ball and usually a stronger throw. However, there are times that this can't be accomplished, so learning how to make a backhanded play (even for middle infielders) is important. Again, we teach the crossover move to approach the ball. Then the key to fielding with the backhand is to make sure the fielder gets low enough on her backside. The right knee on a backhand play, for a right handed throwing fielder, should be on or near the ground upon fielding the ball. Another tip is to make sure the backhand is fielded in front of the left foot and that the fielder is using soft hands (giving) when receiving.

Throwing after Fielding

Upon cleanly fielding the ball, using the right foot / left foot approach for a ball hit directly at the fielder, we then encourage her to transition into a proper throwing position by using the right foot / left foot technique. During our drills we are often heard saying, "right foot, left foot, catch, right foot, left foot, throw." This is easy for your players to remember and many of my former players have told me that they still remember the "*chant*," as they call it.

After fielding the ball, it's important that your player steps with the right foot perpendicular to her body to turn her front shoulder to the target then step forward in that direction with the left foot while throwing. An important reminder for your players is to make sure that the first step is taken *in front* of their body. For some reason, many players will want to take that step behind their body, thus taking their momentum away from their intended target. This footwork works extremely well and looks smooth for any player moving to their glove hand side, provided that they throw with their right hand. Because of that, we will later incorporate a jab-step move for our fielders, so that they can "round" the ball that is hit directly at them.

This is an advanced skill, but it can be taught, and it will greatly improve your fielder's ability to smoothly transition from fielding to throwing. For any ball that is hit sharply at a middle infielder, we teach them to take their first step (right foot) to the right of the ball, and then move back through the ball with the left foot, fielding it off the inside of that foot, and then transitioning into their proper footwork to deliver a throw.

It can be difficult to make a strong throw after fielding with the backhand, but we commonly teach two different techniques. One, we call a "rebound" technique. With this we want the fielder to just raise up from the catch, pivot strongly and throw. This requires a fairly strong arm, but it is the quicker of the two techniques. The second technique is a step through move. Upon fielding the ball we tell our players to step through with the back foot, which would be the right foot for right handed throwers, plant it, then turn and throw.

Fundamental Breakdowns

1. Footwork – Right / Left Catch
2. Head Down – Pony Tail "Pop"
3. Funnel to the Belly Button - "Soft Hands"
4. Footwork – Right / Left Throw

Variations

1. Glove Hand Side Fielding
2. Throwing Hand Side Fielding
3. Jab-Step Positioning

Corners

Ideal corner infielders should possess good reflexes. Because of the short game these players have to play relatively close to the action. We generally slide our corner infielders a full 10-15 feet in front of the bag. Depending on personnel with any given season, we may adjust that. In regard to a *third baseman* who can cover a little more ground, we might allow her to play a step or two deeper than someone who doesn't cover as well. We might use this same approach in an opposite manner with concerns to a slower first baseman. In such a scenario, we would want her to play a little deeper because otherwise she may have trouble finding her way back to the bag to get positioned to receive a throw.

We want our corner infielders to play low to the ground. In fact, our rule on each pitch is that our corners must be in a squat position with the tip of their gloves in the dirt, with both thumbs up. This allows them to play the ball that gets to them very quickly. In their positioning, we also allow them one move laterally in both directions.

For a third baseman, she should be able to pivot on her right foot, crossing over with the left, and be able to cover to the foul line with a backhand. For a first baseman, she should be able to cover to the foul line in one move, as well as covering one move to her right with the backhand. Again, we want players who possess quick reflexes; they do not necessarily have to possess the quickest feet.

Drills

Short Hop Drill

This is a partner drill. One partner kneels on one knee 6-8 ft in front of her fielding partner, who is standing in front of a screen or fence. The kneeling partner is asked to make a short-hop throw in front of the fielder. The toss itself can be difficult to master, but we've had luck by asking the thrower to try to **"skip"** the ball to her partner. The fielding partner should have her rear-end down, glove in the dirt, both thumbs up, ready to dig any throw. We instruct her to move the glove forward to **"scoop"** or **"dig"** out the *short hop*, working it from the ground upward. After 30 seconds or one minute, they should switch.

Reaction Drill

This is another partner drill. One partner stands 6-8 ft in front of her fielding partner, who is again standing in front of a screen or fence. The standing partner is asked to make challenging throws in the direction of her partner. The throws need to be in a variety of directions and need to be made with fair velocity to challenge their partner to react quickly. The fielding partner should be in an athletic position with both thumbs pointing upward. In doing so, she has a half turn with the glove on a high throw or a low throw.

This is important because we want her to be able to react as quickly as possible to any throw. After 30 seconds or one minute, they should switch.

Pepper Drill

This drill can be done with a coach or with a partner. Use some degree of caution, since this drill can be dangerous if not done properly. The coach or partner will stand 10-20 ft, depending on the skill of the player, in front of the fielder and bat the ball in her direction. We ask the fielder to use her corner technique in her set-up and apply the skills taught in the short hop drill or reaction drill. After each ball is fielded, it can be tossed to the side to a partner waiting to participate, or to a bucket. We use a partner standing with an empty bucket; she will fill the bucket with the fielded balls then exchange it with a coach when he empties his bucket. This allows the drill to move at a steady pace. Let the drill move at a pace you feel comfortable with. With our seasoned players, we have a lot of fun with this drill and it moves at a rapid pace.

Backhand Drill

We use this as a partner drill. We make use of the foul lines, having our fielder position herself one crossover pivot move away from the line. Her partner, standing 10-15 ft in front of her, will roll balls at the appropriate speed directly down the foul line. We ask our fielder to use the proper set-up technique then to pivot and crossover and use the backhand technique to field the ball. Upon cleanly fielding it, we then have her use either the step through move and set her feet, or the "rebound" technique where she bounces up and pivots back into a throwing position. Both techniques are fine, and, depending on your personnel, you may want to experiment to find out what works best. After 30 seconds or one minute, they should switch.

3Rd Basemen

"3rd Basemen should have a fearless approach to the position."

~Glenn Moore, Baylor University

Players who wish to play this position should not only possess good reflexes, but they should also have a strong and accurate throwing arm. Because of the short game, and the number of bunts this person will field, you truly need someone who is reliable. Quick hands are a must for this position, although quick feet are also an overlooked characteristic of a good third baseman. My philosophy has been to use my backup shortstop at third base. They haven't always looked like the prototypical third baseman, but they've performed extremely well. The athleticism that a backup shortstop provides allows you to play the corner position a little different in terms of positioning creating a nice wall of defense on the left side of an infield.

Drill your 3rd basemen on how to approach a ball, then how to set their feet and throw. We do this in a variety of ways; however, initially, a good way to do this is to stagger two or three balls in front of your third base person and ask that they approach, pick up, and throw each of the balls to first base as quickly as they can. This will provide you with some immediate feedback to see what they instinctively do well and what they need to improve upon. We ask that our 3rd basemen jab step with their right foot if possible, and then field it off the inside of their left foot before stepping through the ball upon throwing it to first base. This sort of instruction provides them with good footwork and aligns them for a strong and accurate throw to first base.

Tip for 3rd basemen:

Make your 3rd basemen move considerably during any solo work. We like to isolate players by position. We ask that our third basemen get an extra bucket or two of repetitions every day – whether that's before or after practice or during a drink break.

This is a non-throwing drill as we ask her to toss the ball into foul territory after fielding. Require her to move forward to field a bunt then sprint back to reposition before you hit another ball. Then hit the next ball down the line to see her backhand, another into the whole, then one hard shot right at her. Repeat the cycle several times until your bucket is empty.

1st Basemen

Ideally, you want your best receiver outside of your catcher to play first base. Other than the pitcher and catcher, she will touch the ball more than any other player. Therefore, again using my philosophy of ranking importance by the number of touches, this person is extremely important. We need her not only to play the short game, but also to be skilled enough to get her feet set and receive all sorts of different throws. This requires her to be fairly agile, teachable, and athletic. I've never believed in putting my biggest kid at first base just because she didn't fit at any other position. Therefore, I've made it a practice to put one of my most athletic kids at first base regardless of size.

I challenge you to compare two different players at first base during any given practice, one larger and one smaller but more athletic. I can guarantee you that the smaller more athletic player will be at least as effective at receiving throws. The other advantage you gain with the more athletic choice is that you then can position your team differently against the bunt and slap. This flexibility with athleticism on your infield can pay huge dividends defensively.

Tip for 1st Basemen:

So many times during infield cycles a solo first baseman will stand at the bag and receive every throw without ever replicating the necessary skills that we ask her to do in a game.

Therefore, rotate two first basemen during your basic infield cycles. Stress that they have to play the position as it is played in games, up the line, butt down, glove in the dirt – making them drop step while opening up to the field, requiring that they find the bag on every throw.

Middle Infielders

We want our kids who move the best laterally to play up the middle for us. These aren't necessarily your fastest kids. There is truly a difference between lateral quickness and vertical speed. We try to determine our laterally quickest kids in our pre-season conditioning week, using cone and dot drills. Usually, we will generate three to four candidates who can fill our middle positions. Now, just because they can move well laterally, that doesn't mean that they can catch the ball. Therefore, it's important to generate a pool of candidates who can operate up the middle for your team.

Ideally, we'd like to use the player who moves the quickest laterally in combination with the strongest throwing arm to play shortstop. At second base we want a person who can move well laterally and also one who can receive a throw well. Due to the short game, our second base person has to adequately be able to receive throws. Also, because of how we position our corners, it's imperative that we have middle infielders who can really cover a vast amount of ground side to side.

We want our middle infielders to play like tennis players in terms of posture – standing more upright prior to the pitch and then stepping towards the batter, right foot first, into an athletic position that mirrors a tennis player or linebacker's stance. Using the same philosophy we apply to our pitchers, in terms of concentration, we ask the same of our other players, particularly our middle infielders. They, too, should take a vacation between pitches. But for them we describe their vacation as a "physical vacation" because we want them to relay situations and outs between each pitch to the other players. In other words, we want their mouths to be active. But we don't want them to keep the same posture with each pitch. In fact, we require that they constantly change, using the aforementioned technique of being upright and then stepping forward with each pitch into an athletic position.

Drills

Fundamental Fielding

This is a breakdown drill in which individuals will work on their approach to the ball. Mechanically, this is a very methodical drill and we expect to see players performing perfect technique as described above. This can be done with a partner or with a coach.

Cone Drill

We use two cones placed about 10' apart and the fielder is placed in the center between the cones. A coach or teammate will roll balls toward the cones alternating with each toss. The player has to move laterally and maintain proper technique. Once the fielder becomes fatigued or her mechanics break down, then we switch.

Partner Ground Balls

We do this everyday in practice, making use of the entire infield. This drill can be done strictly as a fielding drill, or it can be used as a fielding and throwing drill. Partners space themselves about 10-30 feet apart and challenge each other with a variety of ground balls. We want to see balls thrown in every conceivable way so that the fielder can get repetition using various types of fielding mechanics.

Two-Line Challenges

This drill involves coaches rolling ground balls from the center of the diamond to two lines; one line at the shortstop position and the other in the second baseman's position. When the fielder successfully fields the ball, she quickly tosses it back to the coach and returns to the back of the line. Balls should be rolled so that they challenge the fielder; diving usually becomes a part of this drill.

Shortstop

We ask our shortstop to be our voice on the team. We want her to be cerebral as well as athletic. Some seasons we've been more blessed than others! Any calls we make from our dugout should be echoed by the shortstop; we want her to voice situations, as well as update everyone as to the number of outs. Typically, our shortstop is our most athletic player; most seasons she's also been one of our best players. Even with the other teams that we play against it isn't unusual to see their best player playing shortstop. This isn't by accident; there are some inherent responsibilities that the position demands.

Shortstops have to move well laterally and during the course of a game will often have several opportunities to make plays on ground balls. Thus she must be a reliable fielder and thrower in addition to being able to move well side to side. Other typical responsibilities can include being a primary cut-off for outfielders and a receiver of throw downs from the catcher on stolen base attempts. Perhaps the number of things we ask our shortstops to do leads us to always put our best player in that position.

Drill your shortstops on how to approach a variety of balls. Playing the proper angles is such an important skill that shortstops have to learn. Also, teach them the proper way to receive balls on throw downs from the catcher. We ask our shortstops to straddle the bag and allow the ball to travel as far as possible before applying the tag. It's also important to teach her how to receive throws from different points on the field. When receiving a throw from the second baseman or from any position in the outfield, we ask her to take it from the back side of second base. For a throw coming from the pitcher, or a corner she takes it in front of the base.

It will also benefit you to teach your shortstops how to properly throw or toss the ball in different situations. This works the same for your 2nd base people as well. Teach them how to properly toss the ball underhanded in a close-to-the-bag scenario. Make sure that they always step through their toss so that they don't lift it over their partner's head. Backhanded tosses are rare but not extinct. A shortstop fielding a ball in the hole may need to backhand toss to 3rd base or she may field a ball behind 2nd and need to make a backhanded toss to the bag; therefore it's beneficial that she knows how to do it. She should also be shown how to set her feet after fielding a backhanded play so that she can make a strong and accurate throw across the diamond to 1st base.

Tip for Shortstops:

Have your SS field balls hit with varying velocities. You want to teach her the proper angle and approach to any given ball. For example, balls hit hard up the middle will require her to take a deep arced approach; conversely, a soft hit ball up the middle will require her to charge at a sharp angle.

2nd Base

2nd Base personnel are really similar to your shortstops. They should move well laterally, possess a good deal of athleticism, and should be able to handle a variety of throws. The biggest difference in responsibilities revolves around covering 1st base in bunt coverage. Generally speaking, most teams will move their 2nd baseman to cover 1st, since their 1st baseman has moved forward to play the bunt. To have someone who can handle a throw while maintaining contact with the bag is vitally important. Often times these are bang-bang plays which makes the reception of any throw in this situation pressure-packed. Experienced, athletic players make the best 2nd basemen, but if that combination isn't available, you should go with an experienced player. You'll be better off using someone who won't be rattled when receiving a crucial throw in a tight situation.

Your 2nd baseman will likely use more tosses than any other player on the field. Therefore, it isn't as important for her to possess a strong throwing arm, although you may use her in cut-off situations with the right fielder if she does possess a strong arm; however, you can also use your first baseman or even your shortstop if needed, in that situation. Because of the mostly short throws that your 2nd baseman will make, it's important that she can accurately do so, but also, she must know how to toss the ball properly.

Tosses should be practiced as mentioned in the shortstop section. The 2nd baseman will make more tosses than any other player on the field because many of her plays will be made on the move, and her momentum will take her towards a bag. This isn't true in every scenario; the player can be taken away from the bag she needs to throw to, thus requiring a strong armed throw. Also, a short over-handed throw will have to be used often with this position. We ask our 2nd basemen to use a dart throwing motion to make this throw. This analogy seems to instruct them well on how to perform this short-armed throwing motion.

Tip for 2nd Basemen:

Work with your 2nd basemen on how to toss-on-the-move. They will have fun learning through repetition on how to transfer the ball from the glove to the throwing hand in one smooth motion. Remember to emphasize stepping through the toss on any underhanded toss.

Chapter 9

Outfielders

I'll use the line that one of my assistants made famous when instructing outfielders of their importance, "If an infielder misses a ball you're there to back them up; if you miss a ball… well, you're just out of luck!"

Outfielders carry a huge amount of responsibility that is often underappreciated. When I was growing up playing little league baseball, the kids who couldn't catch the ball were always put in the outfield. And if you really couldn't catch, then they'd put you in right field! I know this, because I lived this! The funny thing is I don't know that our players' perceptions are much different today. During tryouts every season, I'll have more prospects line up at shortstop than at any other position. In fact, outfield spots are usually pretty thin, and most of the kids who line up in those areas really aren't ideal to play the outfield.

So what is an ideal outfielder? We think it's someone who can think, run, throw, and catch. Because outfielders have so many things to do, we try to emphasize to them that their job is just as important as if not more important than any infield player's. Especially when Coach Lebedz reminds them that there isn't anyone out there to back them up!

We need our outfielders to think about or to visualize what their job is going to be in any number of scenarios on every pitch. What bag am I throwing to? Where's my cutoff going to be? What are my backup responsibilities if she bunts, if she steals, or if the ball is hit deep into the gap? These are all questions we want our outfielders to have answers for prior to each pitch being delivered. They truly have to keep their head in the contest and should be prepared to move on every pitch.

Posture and Footwork

Posture

We've always felt that a balanced athletic position allowing for equal lateral movement works best. I have seen staggered stances in the outfield. I have also seen outfielders in a ready position like corner infielders. However, you should teach a posture to your outfielders that allow them to be in a position to move equally in either direction quickly. Being in an athletic stance, such as a tennis player, with both feet pointed forward to the plate provides this.

Footwork

From our athletic stance we teach our outfielders to drop-step with either foot to track any ball over their head. We do a breakdown drill for this almost daily. We want our outfielders to be comfortable using their feet to position themselves to catch the ball. After emphasizing the drop-step, we will work on making good crossover moves to simulate the proper footwork of getting to a hard hit ball that requires a lateral move. Then last, we work on "hard charges." This is on any ball that is in front of the outfielder where we want them to aggressively pursue it.

Three Types of Footwork for Outfielders

1. Drop-Steps
2. Laterals (Crossovers)
3. "Hard Charges"

Corner Outfielders

How you pitch people, whether it is predominant inside or outside, may depend on where you want your best corner outfielder. For us, we generally play our best "catching" corner outfielder in right field. That makes sense to us because we tend to work the outer part of the plate as a pitching philosophy. Therefore, any hard hit fly balls or line drives tend to be pushed to the right side. If given an option, our left fielder typically is our weakest outfielder of the three. For our left fielder we really look for someone who can be athletic enough to cover third on our bunt coverage, and also someone who is mindful enough to remember to do so.

Both corner outfielders are required to backup throws. Any throw-down situation that we signal from the dugout is relayed by our middle infielders, as all signs are, to our outfielders. We want them breaking hard after the pitch to cover their designated area, in case the throw goes astray. For our left fielder, her responsibilities for coverage also include covering the bag on a bunt when there's a runner on first base. Typically, the third baseman charges hard on the bunt, leaving the bag unoccupied, as the shortstop will cover 2nd. Therefore, we roll our left fielder in to cover. In a bunting situation, therefore, we will generally pitch outside and up, allowing us to cheat our left fielder in several steps.

We tend to reposition our corner outfielders with each batter. What a scouting report tells us, or how we choose to pitch someone will often dictate where we put our outfielders. Some years we have lacked speed, so we just kept our outfield deep and attempted to play everything in front. Other years we've been blessed with speed and played fairly shallow and challenged teams to hit beyond them. Personnel, more than anything else, control how you may choose to position your outfielders.

Centerfielders

When choosing a centerfielder we look at two things; speed and throwing strength. If possible, we want someone who can cover a vast area to anchor our outfield. Combine that with someone that is capable of making strong throws back to the infield, and you've got a good centerfield prospect. Obviously, she needs to be able to catch the ball, too! However, I will sacrifice a little on the glove, to have someone who can run and throw well. The centerfielder will be involved in making as many plays as any of your outfielders. We know this because we've charted it through the season. Typically, our centerfielder will get two to three times as many touches as either of the corner outfielders. And when I refer to a touch, that includes catching the ball, picking up a dead-ball, or throwing it.

Because of what we look for in a centerfielder, we also make her our captain of the outfield. On any ball in the gap, it's her voice and only hers if she wants it. The corners will go for it until called off, but once they hear her call they then must immediately retreat to a backup position. In addition, it's her responsibility to pick up any dead-ball that is between outfielders. She knows this in advance, so there is no hesitation when she and a corner outfielder converge on a ball at or near the same time. Obviously, we don't want a corner outfielder standing before a ball waiting on the centerfielder to get there and throw it. But it is important that players know in advance as to what to do if they reach a ball at or near the same time.

The centerfielder becomes a part of our bunt coverage when a runner is bunted over from 2nd base to 3rd base. Our SS will then cover 3rd for any potential throw, leaving 2nd unoccupied; thus, the centerfielder must make that coverage. There are two other responsibilities we ask of her. One, on any throw down from the catcher to 2nd, we want her aware and stepping forward. We don't want her charging forward, this might result in the ball getting beyond her. Second, on bunt plays when a runner is advanced from first, we like to throw behind the runner that has advanced to 2nd with the SS covering the bag. We then have to make sure that our centerfielder covers the left-center gap, in case of an errant throw.

Outfield Drills

Drop Steps

Players line up only a few feet in front of a coach who tosses the ball over the fielder's shoulder, requiring her to drop step and retreat to make the catch. This drill should make fielders drop step in both directions and can be done as a partner drill.

In-Betweens

This is a communication drill that develops better talk between outfielders. Two lines can be formed with approximately 60 feet between them. A coach standing from any given distance will toss balls in a variety of ways in-between the fielders, who break on the throw. Players then have to aggressively call for the ball.

Tennis Ball Challenge

This is a fun drill that is used with tennis balls and a tennis racket that also promotes soft hands. We do it with a coach standing on the foul line smacking tennis balls as high as he or she can to a line of fielders located in center field. This drill can be done with or without a glove – both of which are challenging.

Two Line Hustles

Two coaches, each with a bucket of balls are located, 60 yards from one another in the outfield grass. Players form a line at each bucket. On the coaches command the first person in line takes off toward the opposite bucket. The coach will throw a pop fly or line drive in which the fielder must catch and deposit in the bucket opposite from where they started. This drill is a continuous circle of movement and it can be a good conditioning drill as well as a good outfield drill.

Catch Football

This is a chance for the girls to play a little football. It usually works best if there are no more than five on each team. The outfield is set up as a football field with boundaries and end-zones. Players have four downs to score, failure to do so results in a turnover on downs. The ball is moved only by throwing and catching it. It is down at the location where the ball is caught. There isn't any advancement beyond where a ball is caught. The kids love this game and it pressures them to make catches while being distracted by defenders.

Additional Insights on Fielding

Heinz Mueller, Phoenix College / NJCAA – Phoenix, AZ

See the ball – catch it out front – always thinking the ball is coming to you.

Amy Hayes, Portland State University / NCAA DI – Portland, OR

Do not flip your glove, be it infield or outfield. Play with your glove hands palm up allowing no surprises on a bad hop. Keep your rear and head low to the ball with relaxed shoulders. Shovel out through the ball with your forearms and take the ball to the top of your shoulder – ready to throw. Shoveling out helps shorten the bounce on the ball, allowing the fielder to be in charge, not the ball.

Ed Lantzer, Lake H.S. – Uniontown, OH

We like to practice defensive situations as often as or more than we practice drills. We feel it's important to put our players in game-like situations as often as possible; this way our players are not surprised and will anticipate a play before it happens in an actual game.

Keith Hauber, Lake Central H.S. - St. John, IN

Everyday in throwing drills we have our players perform quick hands, target throws, run-throughs and fielders receive throws as short hops, force outs, and tag plays.

Terry Graver, Elkhorn H.S. – Elkhorn, NE

Develop soft hands – Quick accurate throws – Field the ball in front of you.

Tom Spencer, Notre Dame College – South Euclid, Ohio

Simple!!! Throw and catch the ball. PERIOD! So many games are lost because of a bad throw or being lazy on the catch. We make simple throws EVERYDAY in practice and if we miss, we start over again. The other most important facet is to throw the ball to the right base. It is up to the coaching staff to teach what the right base is.

Chapter 10

Defense: Special Situations, Special Plays

A person could coach softball his whole life and merely stick to the basics of the game and perhaps be very successful. I can think of two or three coaches within our league who play the game in a very basic way. They tend to make only subtle adjustments in their defensive alignments when facing any special situation. And they also tend to be fairly predictable in 1st & 3rd situations. This doesn't mean that they aren't good coaches; it simply means they choose to play the game in a different way. For those of you who want some ammunition at your disposal that might give you an advantage, this section is written for you.

Bunt Defense and Coverage

With no runners on, and a likely bunt-hitter at the plate

The first thing we want to do is communicate that the batter at the plate is likely to bunt. At times your own kids can be your best scouts because often times they've seen players on other teams during the summer and understand their tendencies. After communicating the possible situation, our corners move forward 4-6 steps, anticipating the play. We also tell our middle infielders, who we typically play 3-4 steps behind the baseline, to move in even with the baseline. The shortstop has to be aware of the possibility that the batter may not bunt, but due to the batter's speed she'll need to charge anything in her direction and release it quickly. Our second baseman operates under the same idea but also has to be cognitive of covering 1st base if the bunt is attempted. We like to show two pitches in this situation to try to get the offense to tip their hand. Both pitches, we want thrown up and away. After the first two show pitches, if the batter doesn't offer or show anything, we then pitch her accordingly, but we remain in our standard defensive set for this situation.

We don't develop code words for situations, or play calls, but I know some coaches that do and their teams seem to execute well. We try to teach our players the situation in advance during practice, and then just call it what it is. For example, if nobody is on, then we say, "Bunt situation nobody on." I think either way you choose to do it is effective; the idea is that your team simply understands the situation and their responsibilities.

Less than two outs, runner on 1st

In our game, this is generally a bunting situation. It doesn't mean that you will always see a bunt, but this is the most common time that you will see an attempt. Our corners are even more aggressive in this situation, moving in a 6-8 steps from their normal positioning. Our middle infielders play within their respective baseline. In the event that the bunt is put in play, our shortstop covers 2nd, our second baseman covers 1st, and our leftfielder moves in to cover 3rd. Typically, we want our 3rd baseman handling the bunt, that's why we have her playing where she is. However, whoever fields it will be directed by the catcher as to what base to throw to. The catcher is the only player on the field who can see the whole field in front of her, so, to minimize confusion, we instruct that her voice is the only voice that is heard in terms of what base to throw to. We want to get the lead out if possible, but that usually requires fielding it quickly and smoothly.

If we throw to 1st base with the 2nd baseman covering, we always want to throw behind the runner. Make sure that your centerfielder knows that she has to cover the left-center gap, or an errant throw can end up in the opposition running for a long time. It's amazing, next time you watch a game take note of the advancing runner on a bunt situation, and you'll see that almost every time the runner will round the base at 2nd. Through the course of the season we get four or five kids out on this play, but that's not the only reason we do it. It's equally effective at keeping that runner from being too aggressive; therefore, it slows her down, so in the event that we make a mistake, it may not cost us an extra base.

Less than two outs, runner on 2nd

You will also encounter this situation in a tie-breaker scenario. Our bunt coverage remains the same as the previous situation. Our corners are tight, and our middles are in the baseline. The only difference is in the responsibilities for base coverage. Our 2nd baseman still covers 1st base, however, our shortstop will now cover third for a possible tag play. The centerfielder has to dart in from her position to cover second base so that all bases are then covered. The only time we throw to third in this situation is if the ball is bunted sharply at the pitcher or one of the corners. The exception to this is if the ball is deadened in front of the plate and the catcher is able to field it quickly. A lot will depend on the speed of the runner at 2nd base as to what you'll be able to do, but to avoid a big inning you should make the play at 1st unless you've got a high probability of an out at 3rd.

Less than two outs, runner at 3rd

A lot depends on the inning, the hitter, the runner, and the score. It's hard to predict a squeeze play and when it might be used. Obviously, late in a game with the score tied or with only a run of separation, a good bunter at the plate with a fast runner at third, then there's likely a chance for the squeeze! However, the most effective squeezes are those that catch you by surprise. In the 2002 state championship game, we used the squeeze play in the 1st inning, with our cleanup hitter at the plate. Fortunately for us, it worked, but mostly because it caught the other team by surprise. Because of the element of surprise, we instruct our team to be aware of a squeeze every time a runner reaches third with less than two outs. We won't sacrifice positioning to defense this situation, but we make sure we communicate "squeeze" all over the infield, so if nothing else, it may make the opposition think twice about doing it.

In the event that they do attempt the squeeze, we sell out to make the play at the plate. We don't want anyone to execute this against us, so we practice fielding the bunt barehanded and tossing on the move to the plate. We typically do this drill within our own bunting drills, so the drill acts as both an offensive and defensive drill. Corner spots, your pitcher, and your catcher have to be well drilled to execute squeeze defense. And with the number of close games good teams will play during the course of a season, having a good squeeze defense will prove beneficial.

Slap Defense

We don't have a special alignment for a slap defense as I have seen some teams apply. The only thing that we do is basically have our infield in their basic bunt defense. We then play the situation the same, accordingly, with runners on. The only differences with a slap hitter are that we instruct our corners to not be overly aggressive in attacking the ball, and we have our middle infielders move one to two steps in front of their respective baselines. Additionally, if she's a true slapper, we will move our outfielders in near the edge of the infield.

Insights Regarding Defense v. Bunts / Slaps

Scott Howard, Liberty High School – Liberty, MO

Our philosophy on bunts and slaps is "thank you." In our players' minds, a bunt or slap is an out. Yes, we have given up a hit once in a while on a slap or bunt, but it is not very often. If it's a situation with a runner on 1st, our first priority is to get the force at second. If our fielders have to reset at all, then we get the out at one. One thing that we sometimes do with runners on 1st and 2nd is to have our third baseman play at the bag and let the pitcher cover that side on a bunt and try to get the force at third.

In terms of covering the slap, we simply pull our shortstop and second baseman in by the circle, first base is covered at the bag by the first baseman, third is creeping in some, and the outfielders come to the edge of the grass.

Ed Lantzer, Lake High School – Uniontown, OH

Depending on the score and situation, with a runner on 3rd base, we will ignore her to bait her, pump fake the throw to first, and then throw the runner out trying to score from 3rd. With a runner on first, we will throw the bunter out at first, and then quickly throw to our SS covering 2nd to try and tag the runner out casually rounding the base. Our leftfielder is responsible for covering 3rd base if the runner tries to go from 1st to 3rd on the bunt.

Versus a proven lefty slapper, we like to move our 2nd baseman in near the pitcher, keep our 1st baseman even with the bag, and also move our outfielders in a few steps as well to prevent the dink hit over the infielders' heads.

Amy Hayes, Portland State University / NCAA DI – Portland, OR

Slap Defense: *SS stays home- if there's a runner on 1st, then the 2nd baseman will cover the steal. Everyone else plays normal "D" and reads the hitter for either a slap or bunt. 1B will have to get back if there's a slap and she will cover the bunt if there's a bunt. You must have a first baseman with good feet and an assertive/ communicative 2nd baseman.*

Bunt Defense: *Read the hitter. We will bring corners, pitcher and catcher in to cover the bunt. SS/2nd need to stay home until the ball is down. If we have a strong fielding pitcher then we may leave a corner back, but usually we bring them all.*

Glenn Moore, Baylor University – Waco, TX

***In bunt situations**, defensively we work hard on very aggressive corners and look to get the lead runner always. If we can't we will still have time to get the batter.*

***Our slap defense** is determined by the position of runners on and the location of the pitch. We play the percentages and keep corners back in situations that make a bunt to them very difficult. That will allow for easier bag coverage on steals.*

Terry Graver, Elkhorn High School – Elkhorn, NE

We always have the same bunt coverage; our 1st baseman and 3rd charge along with the pitcher. The catcher gets the balls directly in front of the plate. The catcher calls whose ball it is. The 2nd baseman always covers 1st. Our shortstop slides slightly to 2nd base but then works her way to 3rd in case the pitcher or 3rd baseman forget to cover third. We always throw the ball to first base to get the out. We never attempt to get a runner at 2nd or 3rd base. We want outs!!!

1st & 3rd Situations

So much of our game is contingent upon situation and score, so how we approach 1st & 3rd situations are no different. We do implement a number of plays as the season transpires. Although we are fairly conservative in allowing the runner at 1st to advance to 2nd, but we don't always issue a free pass. We have three plays that we put in. The call is always signaled in from the dugout to our third baseman who then relays the play to everyone else. Typically, we use a color to signal what we're going to do. Here are our three calls v. a 1st & 3rd situation:

Purple - The catcher will bounce up and throw hard back to the pitcher, who has already positioned her body, with her toes pointed to 3rd base, to make a snap throw behind the runner with our 3rd baseman covering.

Gold - The catcher throws towards 2nd base with the shortstop covering, giving the impression of a throw-down. However, our 2nd baseman will cut off the throw in front of the bag and then quickly throw behind the runner at 3rd if the runner is off the bag and not advancing to the plate, or she will throw home in an attempt to throw out the advancing runner from third.

Green - Again the catcher will throw to 2nd base with the shortstop covering, the 2nd baseman will still be in a cut-off position between the pitcher and 2nd base; however, she will allow the ball to travel through.

Each play has its own advantage and disadvantage associated with it. Whatever you use with your team to defense a 1st & 3rd situation, it's best to know your personnel and understand what they are capable of doing. Whenever you choose to implement any special play, understand there is a chance things can go terribly wrong. The best advice is to always be mindful of the score and situation and make sure the gamble is worth the risk.

More Ideas regarding 1st & 3rd Situations

Janice Esses, Bethany College – Lindsborg, KS

We usually bring our second baseman in behind our pitcher to cut the throw from the catcher and have our shortstop cover second. Initially it is the catcher's responsibility to read what the base runner at 3rd base is doing. If the base runner at third has a big lead, then we want our catcher to pick her off at third. If the base runner breaks for home, then the second baseman should cut the throw from the catcher and throw the ball home or to the 3rd baseman, depending on what the runner does. If the baser runner at 3rd base does not break for home, then the second baseman should let the ball go through to the shortstop covering 2nd base.

Keith Hauber, Lake Central H.S. – St John, IN

We throw hard to the pitcher (high), throw to second, fake to second and throw to 3rd, throw to second baseman behind the mound.

Amy Hayes, Portland State University / NCAA DI – Portland, OR

Our SS will cover the bag, usually, and the 2nd baseman will be expected to make the read on the runner at third. (Cut or no Cut) It will always depend on the game situation (inning/outs), but we leave the decision making up to the 2nd baseman who will also be tuned into her teammates' communication.

If there is a slapper up, we may swap that and then it becomes the SS decision to cut and 2nd will cover the bag. We encourage the kids to play the game and react to the situation with only a few basic rules to follow. Any time we over coach; we're in trouble as we've then made the athlete dependent on us as coaches.

Scott Howard, Liberty H.S. – Liberty, MO

Basically, we have four options that we will consider with runners on 1st & 3rd (in terms of the ball being pitched). Which play we use is determined by the score, inning, and upcoming batters for both us and the opposing team. In most cases, the play is on only if the runner at 1st breaks for second. Our plays include: throwing straight through to 2nd to get the runner stealing; throwing the ball short to either our shortstop or second basemen (this varies depending on the players) who can either make a play on the runner between 1st and 2nd or on the runner at 3rd; throwing the ball back to the pitcher who can make a play on either runner (ideally, she'll be able to force the runner at 1st back to the bag, and keep the runner at 3rd); finally, we can snap throw the runner at 3rd.

Ed Lantzer, Lake H.S. – Uniontown, OH

We like to do one of three things. ***Option #1*** *is for our catcher to snap throw a ball to our shortstop covering third base, surprising the runner at 3rd.* ***Option #2*** *is for our catcher to throw directly to our 2nd baseman playing her normal position with the hope that the runner on first will run directly into a tag.* ***Option #3*** *is for our catcher to quickly throw the ball back to our pitcher or our shortstop playing in to get the runner at 2nd into a rundown situation.*

Terry Graver, Elkhorn H.S. – Elkhorn, NE

1. *Have our catcher turn her back so the runner at third can read her numbers and then make a quick throw right back to the pitcher. The pitcher then takes a quick look to see if the runner is leaning towards home. If she is, throw the ball to third and tag her out. (This play worked for us in the state championship game, you just never know.)*

2. *We have the shortstop cut off a throw to 2nd base and attempt to get the runner leaning towards home.*

3. *The catcher fakes a throw to 2nd base, while at the same time have the 3rd baseman slide back and receive a throw from the catcher in an attempt to catch the runner leaning.*

Defending Rundowns

When facing a rundown or "pickle" situation, we want to adhere to a few rules that should result in an out or, at worst, no harm done.

Rules:

1. Only three people involved, one of which is always the pitcher.

2. Stay in the same ditch as your partner(s).

3. Be Visible, But Never Pump-Fake.

4. Communicate and close the distance.

5. Preferably make the play at the safe base!

Rule #1 "Only Three Can Play"

We want only three people involved when defending the rundown. How many times have you seen four or five defensive players involved, running amok, and eventually all over one another? I've seen it many times, and that's why I think these rules allow for the most organized and effective defense against any "pickle" situation.

We employ our pitcher, and her rule is to always go to the base where the rundown was initiated. For instance, if a throw is made to 1st base behind a runner and an opponent was then caught in a rundown, we would want our pitcher to sprint to 1st base. Then our 1st baseman, shortstop, and pitcher would execute our rundown defense, adhering to all of our other rules.

Rule #2 "Stay In the Same Ditch"

To continue our example, our 1st baseman now is chasing down the runner, the shortstop is eagerly awaiting a throw in front of second base, and the pitcher has filled in behind the first baseman at 1st base, and the runner is somewhere in between! Whew… Okay, now in order to keep from throwing through the runner, our 1st Baseman (running) and our Shortstop (waiting) must be in-line with each other, or in other words in the "same ditch." Typically, we want them on the inside of the diamond, but that doesn't always happen. It's more important that you stress that they are facing one another, in the same ditch. We have to always keep this as a rule, so that the runner doesn't impede any throw.

Rule #3 "Be Visible, But Never Pump-Fake!"

Demonstrate this element with any of your kids. Ask that one of them stand about 30 feet away from you, you grab a ball, start running at the kid, hold the ball high and pump-fake ten times before you release it. I'm going to bet that they cringe on at least half your pump-fakes and more times than not when you do release it, they'll miss it. Therefore, we implement a rule that you must show the ball, hold it high, but never pump-fake it. It's too distracting, and the only person that you'll fake out is the person you want to catch it!

Rule #4 "Communicate and Close the Distance"

In our previous example I stated that the shortstop was awaiting the throw "in front" of 2nd base. The idea is to close the distance as much as possible, and with each throw we continue to close the distance. The pitcher, covering 1st base, likewise is actually standing off the bag, closing the distance for any return throw. The other important ingredient here is to communicate. We make it a rule that the receiver calls for the ball and steps to it upon receiving a throw. This is more of a directive than anything. It also makes sure that the receiver is ready for the throw, because after all, they've called for it.

Rule #5 "Get the Out at the Safe Base"

We will take the out at any base, but we'd rather get it at the safe base. The premise behind creating this rule lies in the fact that our game is a game of mistakes. Therefore, we want to be overly cautious on any play being made to an advancing base. So back to our example, we would rather our first baseman throw early than late to our shortstop so that we can turn our runner and point her back to where she came from. Now if there happens to be a bobble, a drop on the tag, or any other malfunction, then hopefully we can at least put her back where she started.

Tips for Rundowns:

- Other players can be used as backups, or safety valves, but never as active participants in our rundowns. We truly want to keep it to three individuals; otherwise, we lose track of responsibilities and all breaks loose!

- When making a tag, make it with both hands. The ball should be firmly in the pocket of the glove-hand, and the throwing hand should be in-on-top of the ball, holding it in its place. In addition, we ask that after the tag is made that we pull the ball out and show the umpire.

Chapter 11

Not just Batting – HITTING!

There are so many different styles, techniques, and theories that have been tried and proven. In my grandfather's words, "There's more than one way to skin a cat." I've never skinned a cat, but I understand the wisdom in the metaphor. Kids can be taught many different ways to hit the ball, although almost all good swings share a set of common fundamentals. In some ways, it's like shooting a basketball. Larry Bird certainly shot it differently than Michael Jordan; however, both were equally effective in shooting the basketball, and both styles possessed certain fundamental truths.

Three Fundamentals for Any Good Hitter

1. Balance
2. Hands
3. Vision

Balance

Maintaining an even balance throughout a swing is vitally important to any batter's success. We stress balance in both the setup as well as the finish. In order to achieve this, we want an equal amount of weight to be distributed between the feet which, for most kids, are set shoulder-width or slightly more apart. Some coaches stress keeping the weight back. We believe doing so creates an unbalanced stance and also encourages the batter to drop her hands when initiating her swing.

From our equally balanced stance, we want to take a short and soft stride to trigger our swing, maintaining equal-weight distribution. The stride is nothing more than a timing mechanism to initiate the swing. The old-school thought was that you "take your weight to the ball" (lunging). Doing so will only create an unbalanced foundation from which the batter is attempting to hit. Think about this, if you were standing on a tightrope stretching across the Grand Canyon sword-fighting Zorro, would you do so with all of your weight on one foot?

We preach to our kids to stride early. We want them to have their front foot down and well-established prior to swinging. So when teaching your players to stride, remind them to make it short, soft, and soon. Striding in such a manner will help them maintain their balance and provide them with a firm foundation in which to swing from.

Hands

From this position it's imperative that the hitter's hands stay behind her hips. Many kids have a tendency to take their hands with them when they stride. To properly teach this, compare their hands to a rubber band being pulled back to pop somebody. When does the rubber band pop the hardest? When you pull it back only to ease it forward before releasing it? Or, does it pop more when you simply pull it back, keeping it pulled back before releasing it all at once?

Back to our swing, the batter has a balanced stance; she's now taken a proper stride, and has kept her hands behind her hips. The next movement comes from the hips, since the back hip should rotate to the ball, more rotation on an inside pitch than an outside pitch. After the hips initiate the swing, which has been triggered by the timing mechanism of the stride, then the hands move toward the ball. And we teach taking our lead hand (pull hand, bottom hand) in a "back-handed" motion to the ball, while our back hand (push hand, top hand) takes a slapping motion to the ball. We want our hands to take a direct path *forward first* to the ball.

We want to maintain our back-hand / slap-hand approach all the way through contact with the ball. Rolling forward and over with the top hand will likely result in a loss of power and produce a less-effective outcome. What happens after contact isn't nearly as important as what happens during contact. Therefore, if your hitter naturally wants to roll over after contact, then we feel that's okay; as long as the habit doesn't encourage her to start rolling over prior or during contact.

Vision

Your hitter can be perfect with her balance and her hands in every way; however, if she doesn't see the ball she likely isn't going to hit it. Above any other fundamental skill, we believe a batter has to be able to use her vision to have any chance at success. We often tell our players that hitting a round object with essentially a round object is the most difficult thing to do in any sport. Our best hitters fail more than 60% of the time. So hitting isn't an easy thing to do, and it becomes increasingly impossible when we approach it blindly.

When batting, we operate under the same philosophy as we do on defense when it comes to our ability to concentrate on any one object for any given period of time. Therefore, we ask our batters to look at the pitcher in the face prior to the pitcher's windup, and then the batter should switch her vision to the hip which is essentially the release point. This subtle change will really help give your batter a point of reference to pick up a pitch with optimal vision and concentration.

The head has to stay on the ball during the swing. We think there are many ways to do teach this. More often than not, I'll simply instruct my players to keep their nose on the ball. Some coaches have their batters bite a chunk of jersey on the front shoulder. I've seen others have their chins tucked so far down that it appeared as though the kid was looking up at the ball. Whatever inventive way you choose, just find a way that works. But unfortunately, experience tells me that every kid is different and what works for one doesn't necessarily work for another. Remember to be flexible and creative, there's always more than one way to skin a cat.

Swing Progression

Stance – Balanced

Stride – Soft, Short, Soon

Hands – Behind the Hips – Forward first to the Ball, Back-hand / Slap-hand

Follow Through – Maintain Balance

Vision – Pitcher's Eyes to Hip / See the Ball to the Bat

Mental Approach

To believe in oneself is a powerful strength. However it isn't a natural gift that most of our players innately possess, although that doesn't restrain us from consistently trying to breed confidence among our players. We feed them encouragement until their heads start to swell. We want our players, whether they can or not, to believe that they can accomplish anything. We dare them to dream the impossible and visualize success.

Confidence

Think about your first job interview. Did you walk into the room heart pounding, hands sweating, with your internal voice chattering inside your cranium? I know I did, and I also know that every word that came out of my mouth was forced and shaken. I wasn't exactly confident, and consequently I didn't perform as well as I could have. Conversely, get me with a bunch of buddies over a hot plate of wings and I can't shut up; in fact, I speak elegantly enough to consider running for a political office. The difference is in my confidence, which is directly related to my comfort level.

Find ways to make your batter comfortable. Obviously, your batter is more comfortable facing the worst pitcher in your league than she is facing the best pitcher. Why is that? Do challenging situations erode away the confidence of your team's batters? Would you agree that experience and exposure can increase comfort? I do know this: I was much better in my fourth job interview than my first.

We certainly believe that confidence and comfort are directly linked. Therefore, we challenge our kids in practice everyday. We pressure them in hitting situations, we even require certain productivity; otherwise, they face consequences. If high speeds affect the confidence of some, then we move the pitching machine far in front of the circle and we crank it up until they've had enough exposure that speed doesn't make them feel uncomfortable. We constantly seek new ways to challenge our team so, hopefully, when they step into the batter's box, they do so with a level of comfort.

Teach Them to React

Stand in and face a pitcher who is going to release a ball from about 35 feet in front of you at speeds that may reach 60-65 mph without the benefit of knowing if the ball is going to break up, down, in, or out. The only thing one can do is *react* in such a situation. One doesn't have time to think this over; it has to be ingrained into muscle memory. So the million dollar question is, how do we achieve that? If I had the exact answer, I doubt that my teams would ever lose another game. All I can do is share what's worked best for us, and how our teams have improved on reacting at the plate rather than thinking.

Clear-Minded Approach

As I'm sure most coaches do, we instruct our players to visualize while standing in the on-deck circle. What we do differently from some is that we teach them how we want this done. And unfortunately, a blanket approach has never worked well for us. Kids are unique in the way they take-in, think about, and process information. For those of you who have ever spent any time in the classroom teaching, you know this to be certainly true. Therefore, you have to discover how each of your players computes your instruction. Find out if they truly understand what you're telling them, and then make sure they can demonstrate it.

In our hitting drills, we often identify things that we want our players to work on to be successful. We ingrain the correction into their minds until they are often able to identify their flaw in their swing before we even have to say anything. We want our players visualizing in the on-deck area what they, personally, have to do to be successful. For example, if their problem is a long-stride, then we expect that they are working on that in the on-deck circle. We require that all of this self-talk be done prior to walking into the batter's box. Once we reach that area, then we are in a "no-thought zone."

"You can learn a lot from a Dummy"

For all practical purposes, we ask our kids to be dummies when they're hitting. We don't want our batters to think, because that will impede their ability to react. Hitting is certainly a skill that requires thought, but not while you're attempting to do it. Most of us, including yours truly, just do not think fast enough to quickly react to unpredictable pitches traveling at high speeds. I think we can guess right at times, and we can get lucky, but we can't be consistently good hitters when our minds are cluttered with thought.

So how do you get your kids to be dummies? For some of us that's a rhetorical question. But, seriously, how do we get them to stop thinking when they get in the box? Most of them have only been taught to think about what they're doing when they hit. I'm as guilty as anyone else, but I'm getting better about trying not to correct and instruct during an individual's batting practice when hitting off a live pitcher or machine.

Doing so is counterproductive. I agree, corrections have to be made and instruction has to be given. But, it should be done at the appropriate times, such as before or after a hitting session, during breakdown drills, soft toss, tee-work, or any other offensive drill. Otherwise, you're telling kids to do one thing and teaching them to do another. Teach your batters to react and hit without constant commentary.

Buildup Drills

We believe in progression drills (otherwise known as buildup drills). This type of work generally serves to reinforce what we feel are the most important fundamental ideas: balance, hands, vision. Typically, we choose three or four buildup drills before facing any live pitching or machine-work in practice. We start with drill-work that is very deliberate and primitive, usually without a ball, and move toward more advanced drills.

No-Ball Drills

Shadow Drill – Players cast their shadow and watch it as they practice striding. Instruct them to notice if their weight is shifting too far forward or to take notice and see if their head is moving. (Head should remain stationary upon striding) * Indoors mirrors work well for this*

Balance Drill – We ask our team to work in partners. One partner demonstrates her batting stance, while the other partner checks for balance by pushing on her partner's back, each hip and her front shoulders. Upon a positive check, then the batting partner will stride and is once again checked for a solid foundation.

Jump Drill - Instruct your team to assume their batting stance. Upon direction (we use a whistle), they should jump and hopefully land back in a soft balanced stance. We then direct them to stride, blow the whistle, and they jump again. This drill requires that they are soft in their knees; otherwise, they can't jump.

Stride Drill – Require individuals to stand in their batting stance with their front foot approximately 6-10 inches from any barrier. (We use the fence) Have them continually work on a short, soft stride, keeping their front foot closed as they step toward the barrier.

Broken Pendulum Drill – Standing in her batting stance, she should hold the knob of the bat between her fingers, using both hands, allowing the end of the bat to point to the ground. With the bat in the position, it should be centered in the middle of her body, holding it about waist high. Then ask her to proceed to stride and then retract it. This should continue with minimum movement of the bat – in other words, we don't want to see it swinging like a pendulum.

Fence-Swinging - Teammates can line up along any fence. Ask them to hold the bat perpendicular from their front hip to the fence. They should be at a distance in which the end of the bat touches the fence, forming a bridge between the individual and the fence. From this distance the individual demonstrates her batting stance and begins working on taking her hands forward by swinging the bat. If she throws her hands out first (toward the fence) then the bat hitting the fence will provide instant feedback discouraging her long swing!

Fence-Swinging #2 - Have them place their back foot against the fence, standing perpendicular and facing away from it. Again, ask that they work on their swing. This drill is designed to make sure that an individual doesn't drop her hands when initiating her swing. Upon doing so, the bat will immediately hit the fence precluding the swing.

Step, Hip, Hands - This is our breakdown drill to emphasize our swing progression. Your team should scatter about the infield and draw themselves a "cheat." It's nothing more than a horizontal line with three intersecting vertical lines on it. The back-end of it represents where the back foot is to be placed, the next intersecting line indicates where the front foot starts in the stance, and the front-end shows them where they should stride to. Standing on their "cheats" in their batting stance, they may work individually at stepping, then methodically turning the hip before bringing their hands through with a swing.

A variation of this drill involves a coach and a whistle. Each time the coach blows the whistle, it indicates a step in the progression. We do this at a varying pace to see who cheats with their hands. It can be done without a whistle if you wish to shout the cadence, "Step – Hips – Hands!"

Tee-Work

Standard - There are many good tees that are on the market today, some of which place the ball beyond the front of the plate where contact may be made. Whatever tee you're working with, make the contact point relevant to the location of the ball. If you don't have a tee that gives you the flexibility of moving the contact point, then use a throw-down home plate as a point of reference and work your tee around it.

Inside Pitches - Place the contact point far in front of the batter and encourage your player to keep her hands inside the ball.

Outside Pitches – Place the contact point on the front-outer edge of the plate or just behind it. Encourage your players, to swing "inside-out," asking that they continue to take their hands forward first. We have had some success in using phrases such as, "hit it off your back hip" or "look the other way."

Step, Hip, Hands Tee-Drill – Using the same cadence as explained above, we add a ball. This offers visual feedback to this activity and also adds the element of vision into the equation. Variation: Ask them to freeze upon follow-through so that you can check for proper mechanics and balance.

Rhythm Tee – Drill– Using a tee, place it several paces ahead of your team who have formed a line. (If you have more than one tee to facilitate this drill it provides more repetition.) Teammates will take turns approaching the tee with a ball placed upon it, stepping into their stance, striding, and swinging in a non-stop rhythmic motion. The drill is continuous until the "ball-placer" runs out of balls. We use soft-toss balls, machine balls, and practice balls for this.

Soft Toss Drills

Standard – We make sure that the toss comes from the front. So often we see coaches who toss directly perpendicular to the hitter. We feel as though this promotes a tardy swing and an unrealistic contact point. When tossing from in front and off to the side, aim for the front hip to feed the batter.

Two –Ball – Using two different colored balls, different numbered balls, etc., give two balls at once to the hitter prompting them which one to hit only after you've tossed them.

Top-Drop – The dropper in this case, stands on a bucket slightly in front and perpendicular to the batter. The "dropper" holds the ball approximately at her own head level before dropping it into the hitting zone. This drill is designed to promote a quick bat and increase reaction time.

Back-Toss – The tossing individual stands at a safe distance behind the hitter and tosses the ball into the hitting zone from behind. The toss should be soft and arced. The hitter is instructed to keep her eyes forward until she sees the ball and then attempt to hit it. This is another drill to promote quick hands.

One-handed Swings – Have the hitter go down on her back knee and stretch her front leg forward to maintain balance. Then only use the bottom hand (pull-hand, back-hand) to swing a number of repetitions, before switching to the top hand (push-hand, slap-hand).

Small-Ball – A variation to any of these drills is to use a smaller ball to increase the difficulty. A number of manufacturers now offer such training aides, although tennis balls or baseballs work just fine, too.

Machine

Take it, Bunt it, Hit it, REPEAT – We ask our hitters to take the first pitch. We ask them standing perfectly in their stance to track the ball from the machine to the backstop. Then instruct them to bunt the next pitch, mostly this is a sacrifice attempt. Last, allow them to swing, before repeating the process for the next three pitches. Variation: At any point if a player fails to execute step 1 or 2, then they have to start over before being allowed to swing.

"MLB" BP-Drill – you need 12-16 players to do this, with a minimum of two coaches. Coaches stand well into foul territory mid-way down each line between home plate and the base. Their job is to hit ground balls opposite of them to a middle infielder, only after the ball has been put in play or attempted by the hitter standing at the plate who is batting off of the machine. This requires some heads, up especially among those patrolling a middle-infield position. Other than the hitter, we have a player to shag for each coach, a machine-feeder, ground-ball fielders at the middle-infield positions, a first baseman, (protected by a screen from batted balls) players long-tossing with partners in the corner outfield positions, and a lone-centerfielder. It takes probably one practice to work out how you want to rotate, but this drill is fast-moving and keeps everyone involved. It's certainly better than the batting practices when everyone stands around waiting for their turn. We limit hitters to ten pitches before rotating.

Bunt Games – We play a number of bunt games using the machine, from working on suicide squeezes to bunting into various areas for point values. Design fun and challenging games that are competitive so that bunting doesn't become a monotonous skill that kids aren't excited to execute.

Additional Insights on Hitting

Heinz Mueller, Phoenix College / NJCAA – Phoenix, AZ

See the ball, catch it out front, and improve bat speed.

Glenn Moore, Baylor University – Waco, TX

1. *We teach a very aggressive mindset knowing pitchers like to get ahead. Know what adjustments to make during at-bats and make them. We want our athletes to want to be in the box when the game is on the line and we create this attitude through designed pressure situations with consequences during practice*

2. *Mechanically we want a very basic stance with good balance, knees slightly bent, elbows down, head upright, shoulders level, and a 45 degree bat angle.*

3. *We also teach "slash hitting" which is highly effective. Our purpose is to eliminate lower body movement (stride) and to focus on contact and timing. We take the stride out and initiate the hands in the forward position. As the pitcher starts the pitch and before the release of the ball the hands will drift back and up (don't allow the hands to leave the body or barring will occur). Timing will be easier and solid contact will occur at a higher percentage than the full stride and swing. We allow our hitters to go to this at their own discretion during any time of an at-bat. Athletes do not accept this initially but will fall in love with "Slash Hitting" if taught correctly. Power will be decreased to a small degree but not significantly. The results will speak for themselves.*

Terry Graver, Elkhorn H.S. – Elkhorn, NE

1. *Attempt to build confidence in every player.*

2. *See the ball!*

3. *Take the hands to the ball.*

4. *Rotate hips and follow through with the swing.*

Tom Spencer, Notre Dame College –South Euclid, Ohio

Our biggest teaching point is teaching the kids to hit the right pitch. Please see the document regarding this in the Appendix.

Janice Esses, Bethany College – Lindsborg, KS

When it comes to batting, I try to watch each player's technique and see how successful they are. I would rather have a player with an ugly swing that can hit the ball rather than a player with a great swing that can't. If a player struggles with her hitting, then I try to help her improve her technique.

In our practices we focus on drills that help improve hitting technique, hand speed and focus. We do a lot of tee drills because you can break down the swing and focus on certain aspects of it and it allows for more repetition. A batting tee will give you instant feedback if a player swings under or on top of the ball. If a player swings under the ball, usually she has an upswing, which may be caused by dropping her back shoulder or hands. We do a lot of drills that focus on driving the hands directly to the ball to help eliminate this problem (lead arm extension drill, back arm extension drill). If I have a player that drops her hands before she swings, I will tell her to drive her back hand (right hand of a right-handed batter). If she concentrates on driving her back hand through the zone, then she will not be as likely to drop her hands and pull through the zone with her lead arm (left hand).

To help players keep their eyes on the ball and not pull their head with their swing, we tell them that their chin should go from shoulder to shoulder. Their chin should touch their left shoulder (right-handed batter) before they swing and touch their right shoulder after their swing. If they pull their head, their chin will never touch their right shoulder.

We emphasize the importance of keeping their weight back during their swing. If they lunge or shift their weight to their front foot, they will not be as successful; especially at the college level where the pitchers have more movement on their pitches.

We also watch how our players hold the bat. It amazes me how many softball players don't hold the bat correctly. The bat should be held in the fingers and not in the palm of the hands. The knocking knuckles (knuckles that you knock on the door with) should be lined up together. The thumbs then wrap around the bat.

Dave Johnson, Rancho Cotate H.S. – Rohnert Park, CA

We teach a linear to rotational swing. We do a lot of tee drills and front toss. Our philosophy is to want to hit the ball as hard and as far as we can on a line.

Scott Howard, Liberty H.S. – Liberty, MO

Our team probably spends more time hitting at practice than most; however, as a result, our team has become one of the strongest hitting teams in our conference. We do a wide variety of batting drills, but we never hit off a pitching machine. I used a pitching machine sparingly in the past, but decided to stop when a few players who could not touch a ball in a game were simply crushing the ball off the machine. I try to avoid live pitching because of the risk to the pitchers. What we do is a lot of "short toss." My assistant and I stand about 10-15' in from the pitching rubber and throw live to the hitters. We usually alternate so the batters can see different pitches each time through. At practice we'll do this with a screen and hard balls. Before games, we do this with Lite Flites. Our kids have come to really enjoy this, especially in pre-game!

We also do a lot of tee work, especially long tee. Long tee takes a little more time having to pick up all the balls, but allowing the kids to see the path of the ball is much more beneficial than hitting into a net. Another thing we'll do to let our pitchers throw live to batters is to simply have the batter stand in. On every pitch, the hitter is required to call 'balls' or 'strikes', and we evaluate them on this. We have found that our hitters are more disciplined at the plate since incorporating this drill.

Ed Lantzer, Lake H.S. – Uniontown, OH

In practice we do a lot of station work. Tee work (inside, outside), soft toss, live toss, and pitching machine. All of our players are expected to know how to sacrifice bunt, drag bunt, push bunt, and slap.

As an offensive philosophy, we stress putting the ball in play any way possible. We like to put pressure on the defense and force our opponents to have to make plays in the field. With two strikes, we want to shorten our swing and make contact, limiting our strikeouts. Our goal is to force the defense to make 21 plays/outs in the field, not from the mound. On the base paths, we want to be aggressive, instinctive, and smart. The more pressure we can put on the pitcher and catcher, the better.

Chapter 12

Base-Running

One of the most important, but often most over-looked, skills in our game is base-running. How many games are decided by one run? On average, how many runners does your team leave stranded in scoring position? Naturally, good base-runners are a rare commodity. And unfortunately, not every player can be taught how to be an instinctively good base-runner. However, through repetition you can develop a number of good base-running strategies that all of your players can adeptly perform.

We allot a certain amount of time within our practices to cover base-running skills. In retrospect, we don't do enough. I can think of numerous occasions in which base-running errors cost us opportunities. So, I'm not sure we ever devote enough time to such a critical part of the game. But, we do start very early in our season implementing what we feel are key base-running strategies.

Key Base-Running Strategies

1. Taking Quick Left Turns
2. Getting a Great Jump
3. Sliding Safely
4. Situational Running
5. Being Aggressive

Taking Quick Left Turns

On our first day of our conditioning week, we start instructing our athletes how we want them to run the bases. Initially, we have them all line up and simply run the bases as we time them from point to point. We document their scores and then move on to some basic instruction about how to properly run the bases.

We start by talking about "*shortening the distance*" between bases. This can only be achieved by stepping on the inside of each base when circling the bases. It isn't as easy as you might hope it to be! Players will struggle to get the proper footing to do this and early on many will hesitate just prior to the bag. We try to avoid this hesitation by talking about "rounding the bag" or, in other words, as a runner, you should prepare yourself to make a quick left turn before reaching the bag

Running Straight Through

We want our players to quickly advance down the line, eyeing the bag the entire way. This is nothing more than a sprint to the finish, without the lunge at the tape. We instruct our runners to never slide at first, it's slower. Also, they are told to never lunge at the bag; this is a safety concern. We don't want our players lunging on a close play and risking an ankle or knee injury.

Taking Two

We want our first base coach to adamantly instruct our runner as early as possible to advance to the next base. The coach does this through both verbal and non-verbal communication, and it's not done just in game situations. Every practice situation when players run bases we have base coaches simulating the exact direction that is used in games. Ingraining this into your player's minds will help eliminate hesitation and confusion.

When taking second, we want our player to be given the opportunity to launch herself in that direction. Therefore, early direction is the key. If the ball has been hit to the right side, we generally allow our players to watch it and make their own early decision about advancing. We do however, still give the first-base coach veto power to reign-in an over-anxious base-runner.

Picking Up 3rd

If a runner has rounded first and is heading toward second, her next assignment is to immediately pick up the 3rd base coach. This is for two reasons: one, if we want the runner to advance beyond 2nd she'll receive the instruction early; also, it's a good habit to get into so that an over-zealous runner doesn't run over teammates when you're fortunate enough to have multiple base-runners.

Going Three

Our rule is to always slide at third, unless the third base coach has given the runner the windmill signal to advance homeward. The reason for this rule is to avoid over-running third base, which is the base from which you can score in more ways from than anywhere else. This is a base that should be viewed as sacred, and we believe it's the coach's responsibility to effectively coach it. Any advancing runner going to third for almost all conceivable plays will be blind to what is going on, and she will rely on her third base coach to make a confident, calculated, and early decision about what she should do.

Home Sweet Home

We have to score runs, or we simply don't win. There are numerous ways to score from third, all of which your players should be aware of. Teach your team these different possibilities: hit, tag-up, wild-pitch, passed ball, fielder's choice, error, pickle, delayed steal, steal, safety squeeze, suicide squeeze, or a walk. Each of these requires some understanding for how the runner performs. Taking it for granted that your kids will somehow automatically know will cost your team precious runs.

In practice, we try to simulate as many of these situations as possible and have our third base coach work individually with runners. One of the things that I do every time a runner reaches third is to give her a brief reminder of a number of possibilities that might occur and what she should do. I also draw a line in the dirt with my foot to mark how big of a lead I want them to get. This is ever-changing with circumstances revolving mainly around situations and personnel.

Base Cycles

We re-emphasize much of our teaching about base-running during our daily conditioning drills. My favorite drill for this is called base cycles. Starting at home plate, a single line is formed, from fastest to slowest. Allowing for proper spacing (usually five steps or so) players sprint up the line to first base, running all the way through the bag. On our field our rule is to run through the bag to the grass. Once each player has made it through first, then they repeat the action running through second, then third, and finally home. The next step in this drill is to run home to second (make sure they pick up their base coaches), then second to third, and last third to home. The progression then takes us from home to third, then eventually, to end the drill, players have to run a home to home to complete the base cycle.

This is an excellent conditioning drill, but aside from that, you can incorporate the instruction of your base coaches while also emphasizing proper running techniques. We think it's a good idea to keep our team physically conditioned throughout the season, and base cycles are one of the ways that we're able to accomplish this. Our field is geographically located next to a long steep embankment, so we generally find time to run up and down the hill a few times, too. In addition, we keep our practices fast-moving and physically demanding. As a result, our teams have historically finished strong, and physical or mental fatigue has not been a factor.

Base-Stealing

In 2000, our shortstop set the all-time record for stolen bases in a season for our state, with 67. She was by far the fastest kid that I have coached and went on to have a tremendous college career, becoming a First-Team Easton All-American in her senior campaign. Last season, one of our players came within one stolen base of the Class "A" record, as she stole 42. Each of these players was thrown out only once in all of their attempts during their record runs. This proves two things: first, each of them had speed that enabled them to steal bases, second and more importantly, we knew when to have them steal.

It's true that you can't coach speed. You can make minimal improvements through weight-lifting, conditioning, and agility drills, but natural speed is just that – it's inherent if not genetic. It's important to determine which of your kids possess enough speed to steal bases and which do not. You can use a stopwatch to try to determine this, but if you do, obtain your data through steal attempts in games. We feel that it is difficult to get an accurate read on a player by how fast they run from home to first in practice. I say this because not every fast kid will be a good base-stealer.

Getting Good Jumps

Beyond having good speed, players need to be able to get good jumps before they can have consistent success at stealing bases. There are several setup techniques that are all good. We try not to have our kids use any one specific setup, but rather allow them to do what feels comfortable, so long as their timing is good. Timing is the most critical component to getting a good jump, and ultimately, stealing a base.

We picked up a drill at a clinic that really helped our players with their timing. You need a pitcher, preferably a catcher, runners and two coaches with whistles. The pitcher is instructed to simply pitch; this drill can be done in combination with your pitcher's workout if you want. The runner sets up in her advancing position and works on getting off the bag "on-time." One coach blows his whistle when the pitcher releases the ball, and the other coach blows his whistle when the runner's foot leaves the base. In a perfect world the whistles happen at the same time. What the drill does for sure is give immediate and recognizable feedback to the runner and her coaches. We think this is a great way to help create better timing for our runners in their attempt to steal bases.

Variations

We also add a first-baseman into this drill (or a covering second baseman), and work on getting leads and diving back safely. You can implement a catcher's throw into this drill which provides more feedback for your runner, concerning her lead. You may even want to rotate your catchers and make it a pitching, running, catcher-throwing drill. We also can add a shortstop who covers second into this drill and work on "delay stealing." The fun part about our game is that there are so many things that you can work on, and sometimes you can creatively work on many of them at the same time.

When to Steal

Being calculated yet unpredictable often yields the best results when stealing bases. The latter of which is hard to do when you're attempting to steal with the best base-stealer in your league. However, as a coach you can discover pitcher / catcher patterns which allow you to catch your opponents by surprise and steal with runners who otherwise pose no threat to steal.

1. Carefully observe the catcher's mannerisms and mechanics. Does she always check runners? Is she lazy or slow in getting to her feet and returning the ball back to the pitcher?

2. Understand the count on your hitter and what pitch is likely to be thrown. Does she usually go off-speed on a two-strike count?

Or will the selected pitch put the catcher in an unfavorable position to throw from?

3. Determining if pitch location will blind the catcher's view. Can the catcher see your runner attempting to steal at first with a left handed batter at the plate on an inside pitch?

You can also take advantage of situations that seem less predictable to steal. We play this way, and, more often that not, it works. It doesn't always work, but I'm not sure there are a lot of fool-proof strategies in our game. After all, it's a game of numbers and percentages; you have to find the ones you're willing to gamble with.

1. Try stealing on the second pitch after a failed sacrifice attempt. The first pitch generally doesn't work as well because an advancement of the runner with less than 2 outs is still expected. With two outs, we may steal on the second pitch and absolutely if the first pitch thrown was a ball.

2. Steal with your cleanup hitter. By definition most cleanup hitters aren't supposed to steal. For some reason, regardless of her speed (even if she's moderately fast), teams generally let their guard down when a cleanup hitter reaches.

3. Steal with two outs. Many teams become more focused on the batter and less so on the runner when they have two outs recorded.

4. Steal immediately after your team has gained tremendous momentum. This can usually be identified when your team has connected on three or four hits or the other team has committed a string of errors. It's an opportunistic time.

5. Steal immediately after the opposition has gained momentum. This usually comes after a great play made by a defender or a strikeout of a tough hitter. It's risky, yes, but they already have

the momentum, so what do you have to lose besides an out, and you just may steal the momentum back along with the base.

Stealing 3rd

Several seasons ago I attended a national clinic in which I observed a session on how stealing third was an easier base to steal than second. The clinician made some very good points, such as runners can get bigger leads, catchers are partially obstructed by a right-handed batter, it's less predictable, and it's a tougher coverage for the defense. There are also argumentative points that can be made: the catcher can easily see it – alerting her reaction time, it's a shorter throw and shortstops are usually covering third on a steal attempt from second, and it's safe to say that shortstops are among the best athletes on the field.

We like for our runners to steal third, but we are more calculated about when we do it and who we attempt it with. Third base, as previously discussed, is the most important base on the field in terms of where we score from. If there aren't any outs, despite wanting to be unpredictable, we aren't going to allow any runner to steal third. There are many other ways that will give us a higher probability of success to get her there. If there is an out, we may consider it, but we want to make sure our lineup matches the situation. In other words, we aren't likely to do it if we have a good run-producing hitter at the plate. With two outs, it's really uncommon that we steal third, unless we're trying to create a mistake by the defense because we have a low-contact hitter at the plate.

Nothing to Lose

There are times with two outs that you should always attempt to steal. These are situations that lay the groundwork for future innings. For instance, perhaps you have your leadoff hitter at the plate with two outs and a runner at first. We would rather attempt a steal with our runner, regardless of who she is, and either have her safely reach second and be in scoring position, or, at worst, she's throw out and we can start the next inning fresh with our leadoff hitter.

I don't want to give you the idea that we simply want to get out in the aforementioned example. We don't want to, but we have more to gain by the attempt than not attempting. There are other situations when we implement this strategy. It hinges on knowing your personnel, what inning it is, and what you want to setup for future innings. Think in advance, and weigh the pros and cons of the situation and then steal if you have nothing to lose.

Hit and Run

The hit and run can be a valuable strategy if you have the personnel to execute it. You need two things, a heads up base-runner and a ground ball type contact hitter. That's the best combination for making a hit and run work well. The good runner allows you to possibly be successful in stealing a base or making it safely back to her starting base on a failed hit and run. We describe it as being failed when the batter doesn't put the ball in play on the ground. Anything that happens aside from that is a failed attempt and if it happens to work out otherwise, then we got lucky.

We feel the best time to hit and run is with two outs. It automatically eliminates the consequences of a double play if the ball were to be hit in the air. The payoff can be tremendous because you start your runner(s) and it causes fielders to vacate their areas to cover bases. Also, it's important to be aware of the count. If the count is in the hitter's favor and the pitcher has to bring a strike or a fastball, then you'll make the job for your girl at the plate much easier.

Knowing when to activate a hit and run is as important as having the personnel to do it. One doesn't want to try it at a time that might completely take your team out of a big inning, should it fail. Remember these are often high-risk gambles that you're taking any time you get aggressive on the bases, and some have better odds for a big payday than others.

Chapter 13

Assistant Coaches, Substitutes, & Umpires

Having good assistant coaches and using them properly can be life-saving. These are the people whom you can and will confide in. They go to battle with you everyday at practice. Good assistants will shield you from criticism and keep you from second guessing yourself when things don't go well. And they can lessen your responsibilities if you let them.

Give your assistants an opportunity to feel a part of what you are doing. Make sure that you ask their opinions, and really listen to what they say. You know that you have to make all the final decisions, but try to reach a consensus with the other coaches on your staff. By doing so, you will be motivating your assistants while also creating a bond of loyalty that every good staff needs.

Roles

Assistant coaches can fill many roles that go beyond hitting a round of infield. Allow your coaches to specifically develop personnel, based upon their area of understanding. If your assistants don't possess a specific area, then ask them what group they would feel most comfortable working with. I've had a different number of coaches for each of my teams. And having a limited number of coaches doesn't allow you to specialize perhaps as much as one would like to. Whatever the number of coaches, at the very least I will assign one coach to the outfield and one to the infield. This allows for consistent teaching during breakdown sessions.

If I have several assistant coaches, I may assign one to the outfield, one to the infield, one to pitchers and catchers, another to conditioning and base-running. If I was ever blessed with more assistants than that,

I'm sure I could make up some other useful task! The point being, find jobs or roles that your assistants can take ownership of. This will motivate them to work harder and make them feel more involved.

Base Coaches

Conventionally, most head coaches will occupy the third base coaching box, with an assistant performing the duties in the first base coaching box. As the head coach, you probably understand your duties of facilitating signs, offering instruction, directing advancing base runners, etc. But… have you ever taken the time to instruct your assistant standing across the diamond from you as to what his or her responsibilities are? Admittedly, I have not always been the best at this. I've been blessed with really good people to work with who often seemed to need little or no direction. However, even as good as those people often were, there were always situations where they didn't perform the duties the way I wanted. And I couldn't be upset with them; after all, I had not told them what I expected them to do. Therefore, take the time prior to the season and coach your coaches on what you want them to do and how you want them to handle situations.

Essentials to Consider for a 1st Base Coach

Use a common language for base-runners.

How to communicate with runners taking a lead.

How they will communicate a missed sign to a runner.

Where their focus is on each pitch in each situation.

It is vitally important that coaches use a common language when communicating with base runners. A runner has to make a split decision on whether to advance or hurry back to a base. Because of this, you want them to optimally react to your direction. In order to achieve this, how you instruct them to do this needs to be the same among your coaches.

Runners who have taken a lead need to understand the language the base coach will use. The base coach then must consistently use that language to teach players to react to his or her commands. Using words like "go" and "no" sound too much alike, so you should find better ways to instruct. We use words such as "back" or "stop" to restrict runners. To advance runners we will tell them the base to go to, ex. "two," "three," or "home."

Additionally, a first base coach may have to relay a sign to a runner whose vision was blocked, or she simply just missed it. How do you want your assistant to do this? Do you want him or her to step to the runner and whisper? Do you want the runner to signal back to the third base coach that she didn't get it? Maybe you want the first base coach to signal to the runner? Whatever you choose to implement, make sure that you've communicated this inevitable problem because kids will miss signs, and it can cost you dearly.

Last, identify what you want your assistant coaches focusing on during different scenarios. Particularly your first base coach, where should his attention be during each situation? To tell him won't make you look like a dictator; instead it shows that you're making sure that everyone is on the same page and that you are maximizing your coaches. When each coach serves a role and performs a duty, your team ultimately benefits.

Substitutes & Role Players

Early in the process, once you've decided on a starting lineup, you need to communicate to the entire team the vital role of the substitute player. Maintaining positive team chemistry will depend on you effectively doing this. It's important that not only the substitutes themselves hear your message but also the entire team including assistants and managers. Subs are important; they perform roles, and they are needed every bit as much as starters if your team is to prosper.

Every kid wants to play, their parents want them to play, their friends want them to play, and frankly, deep down inside you probably even want them to play. But let's be truthful; there are some kids who will sit on your bench and may never play much. This can be problematic, unless you address it early and make every warm body sitting in your dugout feel a part of what you are trying to accomplish. To do so, you have to downplay playing time, and emphasize how important it is to support each other and perform specific roles.

Keep your substitutes mindful and fresh. Have them sprint to the foul pole between innings, or take up a ball and play catch either with an outfielder or with each other in foul territory. Update them on game situations and where they may be used, and constantly keep them focused on the game. If you can accomplish this, then your substitutes will be ready and won't rot away on the pine.

You basically have ***three types*** *of players on your bench:*

1. Players who perform specific roles serving as a hitter, defender, or runner.

2. Marginal players close in talent to your starters.

3. Those who may never play.

We make it a point to find kids who can specialize and perform a certain task. For example, we will strategically select one or two kids who can serve primarily as courtesy runners. We want them to take pride in their role and excel in it. It's amazing how well a player will perform a role if you stress its importance. They soon start to relish their role and become eager to perform it. And by the middle of the season, I don't even have to call on them; they are standing at the edge of the dugout with their helmet on ready to do business. She performs a role, enjoys it and looks forward to her opportunities. She does that because we've continually stressed how valuable she is and her teammates understand it.

In addition to one or two players whose primary use is to fulfill a courtesy running role, we also have a handful of subs who are probably talented enough to play but aren't as good as a starter. These are the ones who push the kids ahead of them at practice and eagerly await their turn. You have to be careful with these because they know they're close. To manage their egos and keep them motivated, you have to play them. And you have to play them in meaningful situations. Allow them to pinch hit in a key spot, substitute them as a late-inning defensive replacement, or make one a designated bunter. Find ways to get these kids in contests because it will do two things for you. First, it will provide you with depth that can prove beneficial as your season progresses. Second, it satisfies those players and parents, which results in fewer problems for you and promotes better team chemistry.

Last, you may have players who you think will never play or contribute in any way outside of vocal support. It seems I've had one of these on every team that I've ever coached. Honestly, some of my fondest memories have come from these individuals. They will surprise you if you give them a chance. You'll find that her teammates will root for her and cheer her on more than any other player. Giving a kid like this an opportunity to play can really spark your team, and it can also be rejuvenating for a coach.

I started a tradition in my first year of coaching. Every last home game for our team would be designated as senior night. On that particular night all seniors would start and play the entire game, regardless. Well, for the first few years a favorable schedule provided us with a cupcake opponent in which the outcome was never in doubt. By year four our schedule changed.

Ashley was a freshman on the very first team that I had coached. I had as much respect for her as any kid I've ever coached. She was always on time for practice; every day she worked as hard as anyone else, but she was never as good as any of the other players. As a result of her lack of skills, she received very little playing time and only a handful of at-bats in her four year career. On senior night, Ashley got her first and only start. The game advanced into the seventh inning, we were up by one run and the opposition had runners at second and third with two outs (I'm not making this up!). Ashley was playing left field, and with our hard-throwing pitcher in the circle, she had not seen so much as a bloop single hit her way all night. Then with the game on the line, the batter absolutely roped a shot to left field; Ashley never moved her feet, only sticking her glove hand toward the ball and surprisingly made one of the biggest catches of the season. Who could have ever predicted that finish? The crowd erupted with excitement; every single player sprinted to left field to congratulate her on the game-saving grab, and each coach in both dugouts smiled mostly in disbelief.

The point of the story is that even your last player on the bench can and will surprise you if you give them an opportunity. And when you see that kid succeed you will never forget it nor will they. And in the bigger picture, creating those memorable moments is really what it's all about.

Roles for the Substitute

Base-Runners

Pinch-Hitters

Designated Sacrifice Bunters

Charts

Signal Signs

Lead Cheers

- Equipment Manager

In addition to the traditional roles a substitute can play, find other ways to engage them. Allow them to chart pitches or other aspects of the game you want more information on. Give them some ownership by providing them with the opportunity to sign-in different plays. Perhaps you give two players the job of signaling in pitches and let the opposition try to determine which one is only faking it. Designate one person as your vocal leader and have her encourage cheers and support. Put two or three players in charge of organizing equipment between innings. There are many things that you can have your substitute players doing besides merely sitting on the bench. And if you give it some thought, you will realize that having them do something constructive will make their time more enjoyable and will benefit everyone.

Umpires – "Handle With Care"

Umpires are people too. Sometimes in the heat of battle, when we firmly disagree with their judgment, we often forget this. And because they are essentially human, they will make mistakes. It is part of the game, and the sooner you and your players realize it, the better equipped you'll be to handle it.

My first trip to the state tournament, we ran into an elderly umpire who was set in his ways and was looking to make a statement. Unfortunately for us, he did. He declared time and time again that our pitcher was making an illegal pitch. Now, never in the previous 25 games that she had pitched in, or in the four that followed this game was she ever called for such action. However, he was obviously seeing something that many other set of trained eyes had never seen.

As you probably can imagine, I was furious. I contested his call each time he made it. His frustration with me gave us no breaks. And my frustration with him didn't allow me to focus on the overall game at hand. Fortunately for us, we were able to play through it and advance. However, the way he and I argued and the position I took came back to haunt me several years later.

I was not nice to him, nor was he nice to me. Our conversations would best be described as confrontational. At that time, I spoke to him without regard for the present, or more importantly, as it turned out, the future. It wasn't until several years later, but we did meet again. Unfortunately, I think he brought with him some of the same predetermined opinions as I had. I felt during warm-ups that we were going to be in trouble because of the cold demeanor he had displayed toward me during the lineup exchange. My feelings were right on target. This is the only time I can honestly say that my team got hosed. And I can't help but blame myself for how I had treated him several seasons before.

I'm not so naïve as to think that every umpire carries a grudge. However, I'm also human, and I understand how people like to be treated. In addition, I know that some people can be vindictive and that some umpires aren't above settling the score when given the opportunity. Therefore, it's always wise to approach an umpire with respect and regard for how future encounters might play out.

One of the most gratifying moments in my coaching life came when I received a Christmas card from an umpire. The card read as follows:

Coach Hardin,

Congratulations on a great season. It is always such a pleasure to be on the field with such great coaches and players. Your team is always respectful and plays with the utmost class.

Merry Christmas - Lane Kugler

This card alone made me feel guilty about every questioning glance I ever gave this man! It also made me feel thankful for the conduct of my players, and it was so gratifying to know that an umpire had taken notice.

We inform our players to never question an umpire. If anyone is to question their judgment, then it will be done by a coach. We ask our players to always be respectful when they believe an umpire to be wrong. We have strict rules concerning this and feel it is important enough to implement consequences for any infractions.

The umpire has a difficult job to perform. We understand this, and we need our players to understand this. Have your players demonstrate their respect to umpires by handing them the ball after a third out or engaging them in friendly conversation during appropriate times. The catcher can really mold a friendship with umpires. She, after all, is his own personal protector, and, due to her proximity to him, she can strike up a dialogue through an entire contest. Don't undervalue what this can do, not only for the game at hand, but for many potential meetings in the future.

Disagreeing with an Umpire

It's okay to disagree with an umpire, in fact they expect it. I spent a part of my college years paying the bills by umpiring baseball and officiating basketball games. Fifty percent of the time you've probably made someone happy and someone else upset. Even when you've made an obvious judgment, coaches and many times players refuse to agree. Most umpires know this, and many have developed a very high threshold for withstanding criticism. However, this doesn't mean that you can persistently rant and rave.

Treat an umpire as you would want to be treated in a questionable moment. Think about your workplace. How would you want a co-worker or even your supervisor to approach you in a moment of discontent? Again, it's okay to disagree; what is not okay is to do it in a demeaning or belittling way. Whatever your disagreement with an umpire is, whether it's his or her strike-zone or a questionable call on the bases, remember to think before you fly off the handle.

There will be moments when you are so infuriated that you will want to fly out of the dugout and sprint onto the field as quickly as you can. Although the speed at which you arrive at the umpire's unwavering position isn't going to better your chances of him changing his opinion. Also, by darting out of the dugout so quickly, you likely aren't going to be able to think about what you say in advance and will become a babbling idiot while explaining your case. So *take your time* coming onto the field, kindly ask for time and then leisurely approach the umpire whom you disagree with. This will give you time to think, and it will also take the umpire off edge.

When stating your case with an umpire, look at him and discuss the issue in a calm voice with clarity. Pace yourself and make sure you are able to truly present yourself. Despite the unlikelihood that the call will be reversed, the umpire will appreciate your style, since it shows a tremendous amount of reserve and respect. Also by not creating a big scene, the fans will be less agitated, the umpire will fully think about your opinion, and you just might get the call to go your way the next time. Think about it; nobody likes to be shown up, especially an umpire whose job is tough to begin with.

Georgia Southern Coach Natalie Poole on How to Question an Umpire

When questioning an umpire, do it with respect. I believe that the umpires expect us to fight for our team, but it does not need to be done in a disrespectful way. I have read statistics that show that a high percentage of umpires do what they do because they enjoy the sport, not because they have to do it strictly for income. The thing that they say worries them the most and dislike the most is how they are treated by coaches. They also stated that when they are treated in a harsh way, it actually distracts them, so what may have started as a simple mistake may get worse because they lose focus.

I feel as though we can state our case, so long as we first know the rules of the game. I can say that from experience because I am respectful to umpires and keep things focused on the matter at hand (instead of anything personal) when I do question them, they listen, stay patient, and are more susceptible to work with me. I think it is important to know what to question and when. It is pointless to question balls and strikes. Also, they do not like to be annoyed with the same issue over and over again.

Chapter 14

Motivation and Leadership

There are numerous books and resources available that promise to motivate your team and make them a stronger more productive group. Personally, I believe that any book you read offers some amount of advice that can be learned. However, the only books that I have come to really depend on are those written by Jeff Janssen, MS. His products are available through his website at *jeffjanssen.com*.

Jeff Janssen has authored numerous books, articles, and videos. His talents have been tapped by top athletic departments across the country including: North Carolina, Stanford, Tennessee, Texas, Florida, Miami, LSU, Arizona, and many others. In addition to consulting with schools, he has also worked with various Fortune 500 companies. His products are great and full of innovative and useful information that can make your teams better.

Team Building

Team Building is constantly under construction and if you take a few days off, then the whole thing might just crumble. Teams are often a true representation of our unique society. It's likely that your team will consist of kids who come from all walks of life, uniquely different from the way they were raised to the demographics that categorize us all. Then you add petty, immature comments that are exchanged between teammates and friends and you start to see the complications that exist before you even have your first meeting.

One of the biggest victories you will achieve is when you bring all of these different characters together to overcome challenges. These challenges aren't only the ones that are obvious, but are also those that transcend our sport. Being able to get teammates to accept others despite their differences so that they can all achieve goals has always been my definition of success. It doesn't show up on a scoreboard, and nobody reads about it in the paper, but you can be assured that it's a lesson that lasts a lifetime with those who are willing to accept it.

Team-Building Activities

We've done a variety of things with each group, and again, as discussed in previous sections, it is contingent upon personnel. For instance, one year we had four kids on our team who were perfect 4.0 students. In contrast to those, we also had about six that were borderline academically ineligible. So we collaborated with our strengths and overcame our deficiencies, which ultimately brought our team closer together. Each Monday night, we held an hour-long team study hall right after practice. We cut practice short on those days, met in my classroom, ate some snacks, and helped each other out. It really benefited our team on two fronts that season, but it wasn't something that every group would have appreciated as much.

Team Dinners are always good activities. Different parents will usually accommodate the team for pasta or hot dogs. We strongly encourage that all team members attend these functions. The environment usually allows for your players to see you and their teammates in a different way, and it can be a healthy way to bring your team together.

Team Outings can be good if you team behaves. We want our team to make sure that they are representing more than themselves when joining a team. Going to a bowling alley, a movie, out to dinner, attending games, or any activity where the public can see you should be done only after your team knows how to conduct themselves properly. Gaining a negative reputation isn't going to do much for your fan base or your job security. I'm not trying to talk you out of indulging in team activities such as these, just warning you to be careful!

Fundraising is also a good way to bring your teams together. Any fundraiser that requires your team to work together in a common place, such as carwashes, can serve your group well. The drawback again, as with any such activity, is you have to make sure that all members attend; otherwise, your attempts will be detrimental. If someone doesn't come, then she will be ostracized in some form. And if raising money is the only motivation for the fundraiser, then I suggest individual candy sales with a system of rewards unrelated to softball.

Daily Activities provide us with our most common and effective form of team-bonding exercises. Jeff Janssen's book, *Championship Team Building*, has served as an excellent guide for finding such. Through a variety of challenges and mostly hands-on activities, your team will have to communicate to solve the problems this resource will provide for them. We used this book religiously throughout our past season, and I have to believe that it truly helped our team develop excellent team chemistry.

Speeches – Rants and Raves

More often than not, I find myself talking more than I should. Invariably, the kids lose their focus and start picking the grass by the time I ever get to my main points. This is a problem. One of the ways we have addressed this is to make sure, as a rule, that eye contact is always being made when any person is talking. (It's also a good life lesson.) In addition, we ask them a series of questions at the conclusion of any speech to make sure that they listened to what we had said.

It's very important to know what you want to say. Keep it somewhat brief and focused. Kids are only going to remember so much, so make sure you're able to key in on those items that you really want them to know. This is true when giving a pre-game speech or a post-game speech. Think about your attention span and how you best remember things.

Your team will grow tired of your voice, so be unpredictable with the length and dynamics of your speeches. Just having some randomness about yourself will make your team want to listen to you more. I think it's important to be consistent in your demeanor and attitude, but not so much in your speeches that you give to your team. Be excitable when you need to, calm it down when that's important, talk loud one time, softer the next, just really keep them guessing and you'll notice that they will pay much more attention to what you have to say.

Big Game Speeches

Your kids know when they're playing in a big game – you don't have to tell them. You also won't need to try to fool them into thinking it's not a big game. Call it how it is, be honest, and say what you think about it. Try not to emphasize the game or the importance in winning as much as you stress what you have to do to win. Remind them of their keys to victory in the same way you would remind them before any other game. Gain your composure and be confident when you speak. Whatever you do, you don't want to convey a sense of nervousness or urgency to your team or they might go out and play that way.

Post-Season Speeches

You can go a long way in motivating your team by constructing an exciting tone for your post-season speech. Whether you're having a banquet or an end-of-the-year meeting, have a polished speech ready to go. Stand with confidence before your crowd and outline your expectations for the following season and what it's going to take for the team to reach their goals. If given the opportunity to give a speech in front of a parent group, do it with great enthusiasm and optimism. Your program isn't going to go anywhere unless you believe it will.

Finding Leadership

Positive leadership is the glue that holds your team chemistry together. Without it, your team can fray into many different directions. With it, your team can exceed the limitations of their talent. Who makes a good team leader? How do you teach them what to say and when to say it? Aren't your best players your best leaders? There seem to be very few natural leaders, and even fewer who are capable of being an effective team leader. Through trial and error, we feel as though we've developed a process that answers all of the aforementioned questions and in the end provides us with responsible effective team captains.

Just prior to our off-season work, we hold a team meeting to discuss workout schedules, weight room hours, and captain applications. In order to be a team captain, our players have to go through an application process. The *application* itself is rather general in nature, but filling it out is only part of the requirement. They also have to obtain three letters of recommendation and write an essay describing why they would be a good team leader.

I allow my assistant coaches to narrow the applicants down to four finalists, who will be interviewed by our coaching staff. From the final four, we will select two individuals to represent us as team captains. Those individuals will receive a copy of Jeff Janssen's book, "The Team Captain's Leadership Manual," which doubles as a workbook. The book is designed to be used in conjunction with a coach to help teach your leaders how to be good captains.

The rest of the off-season, our team captains help organize events and practice using the skills the workbook teaches them. It's a great time to effectively mold your team captains into the roles you'll need them to perform when the season arrives. The true benefit is that you will have provided them well in advance of the season to do what needs to be done. This is much easier than trying to develop your leaders during the season.

Selecting Captains

It isn't always that your best players will be your best leaders. In fact, some don't want the responsibility, while others just don't have what it takes. Also, we don't think that you can put an age requirement on leadership. Obviously, seniority tends to be related to rank, but not always. We have had teams that have determined, out-spoken underclassmen who are capable of leading any group.

We really look for two different types of leaders during our selection process. It is absolute that we find one who is a vocal leader. We need someone who can stand up and not be afraid to speak to the team when the situation arises. That person needs to be diplomatic, respected, and fair. In contrast, we would also like to have someone who leads by example – the one who is willing to outwork others so much that her teammates start to feel guilty about not doing enough. These types of leaders can be quiet and still be just as effective.

Whatever you're looking for, try not to limit yourself to only seniors or outspoken individuals. Go into the process with a clear mind and allow your assistants to help in the selection. Having two, three, or more opinions will make it more democratic and, hopefully, will squash any criticism of picking favorites.

Game-Day Posters

A tradition formed during my first year coaching in Cozad has followed me for the duration of my career. It started simply enough; the night before our first game I was working late at the high school and decided to just put together a little motivational piece to give to the girls. I searched the internet for the perfect picture and ideal quote. I can't remember what it was, but I scrapped it together in Microsoft Word, then printed and copied twenty.

The next day I stood outside my room monitoring the hall between classes and began to give a copy to each of my players as they passed by my room. Cozad High School is small enough that the task of seeing each of my players during the day was easily accomplished.

None of the players really said anything other than, "Thanks Coach." However, they must have liked what they received because just prior to the next game almost every player stopped by my room asking for a game-day poster. I was completely unprepared, but I used my planning period at the end of the day to produce another, and I've been producing them every since. I've used a variety of high-profile sport stories, quotes, action pictures, photos of our own team, and numerous other items that are inspiring.

I didn't know just how much these game-day posters meant to my players until I attended a graduation reception in 2003. It was there that one particular graduating player of mine had an entire display dedicated to four years of game-day posters. It was an amazing collection of these things. I couldn't believe that she had kept each one. And as I began to share my amazement with some of my other players, to the very last one, they all told me that they had kept all of theirs as well. My hope is that these positive messages of encouragement and inspiration will be carried with them for the rest of their lives.

Other Successful Ideas Regarding Motivation

Terry Graver, Elkhorn H.S. – Elkhorn, NE

You must get every player putting the team first! You must get the players to believe they can do it!!! Stroke them!!! "All of us or none of us!"

Ed Lantzer, Lake H.S. – Uniontown, OH

Food! For some reason, my teams always love to eat. We always reward our players with dinner at their favorite restaurant for any type of championship won (league, district, regional, state). We've also taken our teams out for ice cream for winning big league games on the road. Last season, during our state tournament run, I promised Subway sandwiches for any girl who got an RBI. Candy and popsicles are favorites at practice any time you are running a competitive drill.

Scott Howard, Liberty H.S. – Liberty, MO

Making the kids accountable is the best motivation for our team. This is a fine line, though, because the kids cannot be afraid to make mistakes. They need to see that you believe in them. In doing this, I want the kids to give everything they've got – hold nothing back. My kids know that if they have played or practiced so hard that they can't get themselves off the field, that I will carry them off.

Really, though, a lot of the motivation comes from the kids themselves. They want to do well for one another. If you are able to really create and build the TEAM, this will usually happen as a result.

Amy Hayes, Portland State University / NCAA DI – Portland, OR

Give them something to think about everyday. Community service: Let them see the differences that they can make in the world. Be prepared so that practice comes across as organized and useful. Team building activities: rope course, hikes, dinners, get-to-know-you activities. Women like to share their stories, encourage them to communicate their proudest and saddest moments. Find out their fears and set a plan to help them overcome them.

Janice Esses, Bethany College – Lindsborg, KS

We award our players with a Starburst candy after a great play. A "star play" deserves a "starburst." This has made our players be more aggressive and dive for balls because they want to receive a starburst. It is also fun for our players. They help me award players by telling me if a play is "starburst worthy" or not. I got this idea from Coach Hutchins from Michigan, who gives her players an M&M when they reach third base and an umpire in Kansas City who awards players with a starburst for good plays.

Keith Hauber, Lake Central H.S. – St. John, IN

Our prior successes have been the greatest motivation. The two greatest motivators are pleasure and pain. We hate losing with a passion and we celebrate our victories.

Heinz Mueller, Phoenix College / NJCAA – Phoenix, AZ

I have a sports psychologist that works with the team. He is very helpful with motivation. I set goals – Have Vision – Look towards the season as a journey – your players must buy into the coaching theory. Trust is a big word and show that you are unified. Never be afraid to admit your mistakes towards your athletes.

Glenn Moore, Baylor University – Waco, TX

We try to create an atmosphere of excitement each day. We may have had a terrible day in the office but my staff knows when we step on the field, just as we ask our players to do, we leave it behind to play the greatest game on earth. We create as many forms of competition as possible. Competition breeds competitive athletes.

Spontaneous changes are good when practices are very rigid, which mine are. Motivation is a cycle; coaches are just as motivated by their players as the reverse. That's why we must incorporate fun into practice without horsing around.

Chapter 15

Rules and Discipline

There's an ongoing theme throughout this publication – "Everything is contingent upon your personnel." And when addressing rules and discipline it is no different. Some teams will need more rules, while others will require very few. Despite the wide spectrum of differences you may encounter, it's a good idea to have a *skeleton set of rules* that carry over each year. These bare minimum guidelines should reflect your beliefs and allow you flexibility to interpret any such breach.

Developing Rules

When drafting your rules, keep them limited to one page. Nothing will turn your team off quicker than looking at multiple pages of rules that control them in every way. Your team will immediately label you as a stickler, and it will depress their optimism for the season. Balancing what needs to be stated and what needs to be omitted is a difficult task. Sometimes it isn't a bad idea to meet with upperclassmen and allow them to vent their concerns before you decide on all of your rules. This input is valuable and it also provides you with an idea as to what your team is willing to accept.

Rules need to adhere to any institutional guidelines that you may have to work in conjunction with. For instance, our school's athletic handbook outlines consequences for violating any of its rules. Therefore, our team rules have to adhere to the standards that are set by our school. We make a disclaimer statement in our team handbook that states: "For issues concerning other matters not mentioned, the activity handbook will be applied."

To some degree, it is impossible to have specific rules that will cover every situation. So we develop rules that leave some room for interpretation, such as our first rule: "Don't do anything to embarrass yourself, your family, your school, or your team." We think this is generic enough to allow us to apply some commonsense thinking when issuing discipline. And when going over your team rules with your team, make sure they understand the broad scope of such rules. Remember, just because you understand that the rule is flexible, that doesn't always mean that they will see it that way.

We do have a few specific rules. I think you have to have them, since there are certain things you need to take a stand on. For instance, we have clear rules concerning our expectations for practice and conduct for games. Again, it changes each year. For some teams, the rules were written to get their attention, being very straight forward; while others are written as friendly reminders. When reading your rules to the team, your demeanor and *voice tone* can send the message as to how you feel about your rules, regardless of how they're written.

Applying Discipline

The most important thing to remember when applying discipline to any situation is to be consistent. You have room for interpretation, yes, but your team will observe how you handle every situation. And if you don't handle identical situations in the same way, you won't be able to prevent the negative backlash. Your team will accuse you of favoritism, see you as unfair, and you will lose their trust.

Minimize the damage that comes with any breach of team rules. Keep the discipline between you and the violating party. The less the team knows how you've dealt with it and what the details were behind it, then the less they have to comment about it. It's difficult to eliminate all of the chatter that your team will exhibit in such situations, so we feel it's better to give them less to chatter about.

Running is a poor consequence. There is a lot of psychological theory associated with how athletes will develop a negative view of conditioning if you do so. However, our thought isn't necessarily based upon that, but more on the fact that we already condition, and we want to turn something bad into something good. Try assigning a player being disciplined to do something constructive. Today, *time* is the most cherished thing to teenagers. Think about it; what do they ask almost every day? "Coach, when does practice get out?" Kids value time so much when you're occupying theirs. Therefore, when you want to discipline someone, require that they do something to occupy their time that can be useful. Have them run the scoreboard for youth games, be on the field crew for youth tournaments, drag the field before practice, clean dugouts after games, volunteer at the local YMCA on a Saturday morning, clean blackboards or marker boards at the high school (custodians welcome the help), or any other number of things that will occupy their time and doing something more purposeful than testing their breathing endurance.

There is another thing to remember when applying consequences to any rule violation: "Make the punishment fit the crime." Most of your players will admit their wrongs and are willing to accept the discipline you choose – if it's moderately fair. This means that you don't overdo it. Usually when a situation arises that requires discipline, there is a certain amount of emotion that comes with it. Because of this, we never issue consequences on the same day we become aware of a violation. We will take the time to talk to the party who committed the act, but we only address their wrong. Our whole coaching staff then talks about it and makes a decision on what needs to be done. The next day we visit again with the convicted and feed them their medicine.

Shouting

If I have to yell to be heard then they weren't listening. I used to be a fiery coach who wore his emotions on his sleeve. I found out that this worked for some, but for others I was scaring them half to death. I've since changed my approach and have tried to be more consistent with my demeanor. This allows my team to know what to expect in terms of *stability* from their coach. This approach also gives your shouting more credibility if and when you do decide to blow your top. In other words, somebody who is loud all the time is going to face deaf ears after a while.

Kids also like to be treated as adults. Most teenagers already think that they are adults. Therefore, they want to be talked to as such. We know that the way that they act at times doesn't merit such respect, but if you can look past that and talk to them on your level, they will respond better. It's a good idea to make them feel like you are all in it together when facing the challenges of the season. If you yell and shout, you will put a gaping distance between you and your team. And it's better to bridge that gap so that your players can talk to you, so they can listen to you, and so they don't have to be afraid of you yelling at them.

Georgia Southern Coach Natalie Poole on Discipline

I believe discipline is very important. The student-athletes are on their own, many for the first time, so they have a lot of freedom. I want my athletes to have a great experience in college, but not at the cost of their education or hurting their team or other teammates, or at the cost of hurting themselves. I am firm about what is important to me and this team, but I do not want them to feel as though they have their hands tied behind their backs at all time, because they will get good at finding ways around that.

They are all to understand that they are held at a higher standard than the average person and they not only represent themselves and this team, but also this school. We like to think in terms of ***"imagine what you are doing becoming the headline of a newspaper,"*** *and if you are not proud of that then you shouldn't do it. We have rules for drinking, curfew, respect, class attendance, being on time, etc. I have repercussions for breaking those rules. They understand that and know that if they choose to break a rule, then they will be disciplined. I* *believe in being consistent and fair. The athletes can respect that. They may not like the idea of getting in trouble, but they wanted everyone to be treated equal when it comes to this.*

Chapter 16

Drills, Drills, and Thank Goodness, More Drills!

Drills are what make our players become better players. The skills in our game are mostly learned. And repetition is one of the best tools we use to commit skills to muscle memory. There are so many good drills that exist, and I've asked the contributors of this publication to lend their favorites. Hopefully, you'll find something new here or be reminded of a good drill you've forgotten about!

Janice Esses, Bethany College – Lindsborg, KS

We do a drill with our catchers to help them become quick at getting up and to a ball they have blocked. We start with the catchers in stance. The coach yells a command, "block," and drops a ball a couple of feet in front of the catcher. The catcher drops to the block position and then gets up from the black position to the ball as quickly as they can. When they field the ball, they bring the ball and their glove to their ear in a throwing position. Their weight should be on their back foot. They toss the ball back to the coach and repeat. We will go the length from home to first base and then back home.

Scott Howard, Liberty H.S. – Liberty, MO

There are so many great drills. We do some things every practice, like our fielding progression, and any drills we incorporate to vary practice. These are just a few drills we like to do. Many coaches probably already do these – some we have picked up from clinics or other coaches.

Multiples

Put your players at each base, and assign what they are doing. For example, a multiple could be 4-1, 1-2, 2-3, and 3-4. So on your signal here's what happens: The runner at home goes to first like it's a hit; the runner at first steals second; the runner at second tags to third; and the runner at 3rd goes home on a passed ball. You can create any situation you want. Very fast-paced and active drill, plus the kids have to focus on what they are doing.

Hitting Scenarios

For hitting scenarios, all I've done is to create about 30 or so different offensive situations. These can include score, inning, runners, and count. The player draws a card, and then has to decide what to do AND execute. (We usually throw short toss for this drill). It becomes a big competition among players!

Perfect 21

In "21," you have an offense and a full defense set up. The goal is to play to 21 outs without any mistakes (offensively or defensively). If things happen perfectly, then you get a point (does not have to be an out). If there is a mistake, you go back to zero. At 11, you switch teams. This game can be started at any point, for example, Perfect 9.

3-Runners

We put three players at home, staggered about a foot apart. On go, they all take off toward first base. The first runner runs through the bag, the second runner goes to third, and the third runner goes to second. Efficient base running is critical – hitting the bags correctly and taking the best line to the next base. You can add to this by having a coach at third telling the player at second whether to be up, slide, or round – same with the runner coming into third.

Glenn Moore, Baylor University – Waco, TX

One of our favorite drills is called, "Double Bunts" - Back to back pitchers pitch to a screen at second and home; the runners at first get their lead from the pitcher throwing home and the runner at 3rd from the pitcher throwing to second. Runners work on bunt leads and reading "angle down" then break hard to advance. When pitch is taken, work on going back to the bag properly. Bunters will work sacrifice bunts and quick bunts (both lines), then getting out of the box. Rotation is counter-clockwise.

Terry Graver, Elkhorn H.S. – Elkhorn, NE

1. **Four corner throwing** – *divide the team up and put them at all four bases and just throw the ball around the horn. You can have a quick throw – spin and throw – slow rollers – use your creativity.*

2. **Outfield drill** – *Single line – have the player run towards the coach and the coach throws low and short so the player must dive or catch at their shoes. They then must turn and run and the coach throws the ball over their head and then they catch it and throw it back to the coach.*

3. **Ground balls**...*Ground balls...Ground balls... We try to get every player 50-100 ground balls a day!!! Pick it up and throw it to first! Attack the ball and field it out in front!!!*

4. **Catcher** – *full gear on – throw short hops in all locations – You can use tennis balls or softie balls – if you are mad, use a real ball!*

5. **Game situations** – *have kids be runners and go through all bunt situations, 1st and 3rd situations, cuts, tell them how many outs, etc.*

- *Make everything game-like*

<u>*Dave Johnson, Rancho Cotate H.S. – Rohnert Park, CA*</u>

- *Base-running situation drills.*
- *The "Freeze Drill" for positioning on any defensive situation.*
- *The "Two-Whistle Drill" for lead offs.*

<u>*Natalie Poole, Georgia Southern University – Statesboro, GA*</u>

One of my favorite drills is to play what I call "Guts." We set up our entire defense on the field in their positions. We use the extra players as runners. The extra runners will rotate into defense every 6 outs, so that everyone gets the opportunity to compete in the drill. The objective of this drill is to get through 21 outs (the length of a regular game) without making any mental or physical mistakes. The coach is the person standing in the batter's box hitting the ball. If they make a mental or physical mistake before the 21 outs is complete, then they drop their gloves and take a lap around all of the gloves. You can change the discipline to be whatever you choose. If a mistake is made and the team takes a lap, then they game starts over with no out and we go back to the first inning. It is extremely challenging, because they are expected to communicate right, run the correct cuts, and make the right decisions on each play. It emphasizes how any small mistake could cost you a win.

<u>Ed Lantzer, Lake H.S. – Uniontown, OH</u>

Our girls always enjoy playing a game we call "Turkey." It's a very simple and competitive fielding drill. One or more coaches hit groundballs to one or more lines of girls. The girls have to field the ball cleanly (no bobbles), and then make an accurate throw back to a designated target or catcher. The last girl standing is declared the winner. You can use regular or softie balls with a glove or you can use tennis balls with no glove. Candy is always a nice prize for the winner.

Keith Hauber, Lake Central H.S. – St. John, Indiana

- *We have our coaches throw footballs to our players using receiver-type drills to emphasize proper catching technique. If we complete a bomb, the player does her best end-zone dance. (just to have fun with it)*

- *We do basic rundown drills with different starting points.*

- *Hitting drills using a pitching machine in different game situations.*

Amy Hayes, Portland State University / NCAA DI – Portland, OR

Pitching: *Spinner spins. Every pitcher should have one of these or a hockey puck. It's a great tool to help improve proper spin and ball rotation.*

One-leg drive: *Standing on just your drive leg, driving forward while doing a full arm motion and pitch release. Great drill for strength, balance and power.*

Walk-thrus with a partner: *Each player has one ball and they stand about 15 feet apart - One walks forward and pitches while the receiver walks backwards, catches the pitch and throws another ball to the pitcher quickly. Once you have gone the distance of the gym or further, then the roles are reversed and they return to where they started. A great drill for smoothing out one's motion, timing and reaction skills.*

Profiles of Contributors

Glenn Moore, Baylor University – Waco, TX

Number of Coaching Years: 13

Career Record: 353-114

Achievements: 2 SEC Championships, 4 SEC Western Division Championships at LSU. 5 NCAA Appearances, 12 All-Americans.

Basic Coaching Philosophy: Aggressive play utilizing a balance between the short game and power. Motivate through competitive fun. To play the percentages and make the basic plays.

How do you define or measure success? *Success comes in many forms. Coaching success is becoming the "one heartbeat" with athletes who have come to you from all different walks of life and many philosophies. To get in the "Zone" and to know that by a nod of the head she knows what I want her to do. Success means providing society with a better product than I received. Knowing I have helped her develop as a person in confidence, decision making, and humility.*

On Respect: *Having played the game years ago when it was not nearly as technical as it is now; I appreciate how far the game has come. I believe that players, coaches and officials have elevated the game in almost every aspect. However, one area that I feel has somehow lost its place by some coaches is the "respect" players and coaches have for the game and their opponents. Things such as pitchers taken out (with a slide) on an up the line definite out play or stealing, bunting and scoring on passed balls with ten run leads.*

I remember when that respect was demanded and I believe the game was appreciated more because of it. I agree that it is not "my job to stop my offense" but when a team gets its eight runs it is much more satisfying to respect my opponent by not pouring salt in the wound with bunts and steals. I am not suggesting that you make outs and embarrass the opponent but score by putting hits together; not doing so just to pad stats.

Terry Graver, Elkhorn H.S. – Elkhorn, NE

Number of Coaching Years: 7 years Head Coach / 2 years Assistant

Career Record: 203-38

Achievements: State Class B Champions 2005, Class B State Champions 2004, State Class B Runner-up 2001, State Class B Runner-up 2000, State Softball Coach of the Year 2004, Five District Titles, and seven consecutive state tournament appearances.

Basic Coaching Philosophy: Making softball fun while expecting and demanding a lot from the players.

"I love coaching softball, it is a great game! The play has greatly improved in my 11 years of being around it!"

Scott Howard, Liberty H.S. – Liberty, MO

Coaching Years: 5

Career Record: 116-26

Achievements: 2004 Class 4 State Champions, 30-1 record; 5 time District Champions; 4 Time Conference Champions; 4 time Winnetonka Tournament Champions; 2 Time Central Missouri State University Tournament Champions.

Basic Coaching Philosophy: My philosophy is two-fold. First, everyone involved has to believe in the program, the system, the coaches, and the players. Secondly, as a coach, you have to be able to pass the leadership to the players. In some seasons, it may happen more naturally or quickly than others, but it has to happen.

Additional Thoughts: *We are trying to add more to base running. With the quality of pitching, scoring runs is so important. My staff is putting value in base running so the players will value it. It is a great opportunity to put pressure on the opponent's defense, and a lot of times it's pressure they are not used to. Teaching the kids to make decisions on the bases is the key to this. If they can see the ball, they should be able to know their own speed and decide whether they can take the next base or steal a base. There is a lot more to stealing than just speed. Players need to be smart, understand the situation, and know when to be aggressive.*

Another important aspect of practice is to make it more intense. I go around and watch spring and summer practices of various teams, and it amazes me how many practices look more like a social gathering than a practice. Practices need to be fast-paced, realistic, and more intense than a game. That way, when you find yourself in a very intense game situation, your players will be ready to handle it. And yes, it is great to have a "loose" day thrown in here and there; after all, it's very important to have fun!

Finally, it's very important to have constant communication with your players. This communication needs to happen before, during, and after practices. They need to know why you do what you are doing. This helps them buy into the system.

Keith Hauber, Lake Central H.S. – St. John, IN

Coaching Years: 17

Career Varsity Record: 201-24

Achievements: State Champions 2004, 2002, 2003 State Runner up, State Record five straight trips to the State Finals 2001-2005. Indiana Coach of the Year 2003, Record 47 game winning streak.

Basic Coaching Philosophy: Work hard, but enjoy what you do.

How do you define success? *Success is making the most of your talents, working as hard as you can, and making the world around you a better place.*

Janice Esses, Bethany College – Lindsborg, KS

Coaching Years: 5

Achievements: Conference Champions 2003, Post-Season Conference Tournament Champions 2003, Champions of Character 2003

Tom Spencer, Notre Dame College – South Euclid, Ohio

Coaching Years: 2 Years as a High School Coach, 9 Years in College

Achievements: Ohio Athletic Conference Coach of the Year while at Baldwin Wallace College in Ohio.

Basic Coaching Philosophy: Keep it simple. We preach attitude and effort. If our players have a great attitude and always give 100% effort we feel we will be successful.

Heinz Mueller, Phoenix College / NJCAA – Phoenix, AZ

Coaching Years: 16

Career Record: 650-299

Achievements: Four time National Champions NJCAA 2000, 2001, 2004, 2005; NFCA National Coaching Staff of the Year 2005; Nationals Coach of the Tournament 2000, 2001, 2004, 2005

Basic Philosophy: Keep the game simple, recruit talented athletes and have a great coaching staff that is very loyal and hardworking. Last is, make the game fun and attractive to players so that they can hardly wait to play.

How do you define success?

1. *The student athlete gets her degree from our institution.*
2. *The student athlete has received a scholarship from our institution.*
3. *The student athlete has received a scholarship from a four year institution through Phoenix College.*
4. *The student athlete has a great experience playing softball at Phoenix College.*
5. *The student athlete has completed a degree at a four year institution through Phoenix College.*
6. *The student athlete has acquired a job in society and is making a contribution to society.*

Additional Thoughts: *You have to have passion in what you do in life and desire to help other people. The success in my life has been the interaction with the student athletes and staff to be successful in their lives.*

Dave Johnson, Rancho Cotate H.S. – Rohnert Park, CA

Coaching Years: 2

Career Record: 39-8

Achievements: Won NBL (North Bay League) 2004, 2005
Took 1st at 3A North Coast Section playoffs in 2005

Basic Coaching Philosophy: We are teachers of life, as well as instructors of softball. More important than winning games is that these young women become good citizens, that they can expect loyalty from their coaches and that the coaching staff expects loyalty in return. We expect and teach good sportsmanship, we expect them to give 100% at all times and never give up demonstrating a positive attitude to the game and others. Also, that we respect ourselves, our team, school, and community.

How do you measure success? *By learning the principles of sportsmanship, the mastering of fundamentals, focusing and giving effort during practices and games, and becoming disciplined & knowledgeable about the game. By doing these things I think they gain confidence and self-esteem. Our goal as coaches is to help each individual player reach her potential. We define success by performance, not wins or losses.*

Natalie Poole, Georgia Southern – Statesboro, GA

Coaching Years: Four seasons at GSU

Record at GSU: 111-117

Achievements: 2002 Southern Conference Coach of the Year, her 2004 team led the Southern Conference with a 1.80 earned run average, fourth-best in the school record books, and her 2005 team set several school records, most notably the new home run record of 34.

Ed Lantzer, Lake Union H.S. – Uniontown, Ohio

Coaching Years: 3 years as a Head Coach, 9 years as an Assistant

Coaching Record: Overall 72-17, League 35-5

Achievements: 3-time defending league champs (2003,2004,2005); 2005 Division I State Champions, 2004 Division I State Runner-up; 2004 & 2005 Stark County Coach of the Year; 2004 & 2005 Federal League Coach of the Year.

Basic Coaching Philosophy: Have Fun. Play Smart. Play Hard. Play Together. Always respect, but do not fear your opponent. Win and lose with class.

How do you measure success? *I feel a good barometer for any program is the number of student athletes that are coming out for your sport. If you have a good thing going, most kids want to be a part of it. Because of our recent success, our numbers have increased each year. If your athletes are having fun and enjoying a little bit of success, other kids notice that and want to be a part of it as well.*

Additional Comments: *I would like to thank and recognize those coaches who have been the most influential to me. They include: John "J.D." DeMarco – gave me my start in softball. He taught me how to keep it fun and how important it is to be surrounded with good people. Holly (Goodpasture) Collins – The first really good pitching coach I got a chance to coach with; she retired early to start a family, but because of her, I now know what to look for in a good pitching coach. Fred Mertes – Taught me every good hitting and fielding drill I know and I still use most of them to this day. Kerry Kaser- currently on my staff, he is an excellent teacher of the game, very knowledgeable in just* *about every aspect of the game. He will make a great head coach soon. Special thanks to every coach I have ever worked with. I have taken a little bit from each and every one of them. I will always be grateful to them for that. Lastly, thanks to my family. Their support is a big reason why I continue to enjoy coaching. They are my biggest fans.*

Amy Hayes, Portland State University / NCAA DI – Portland, OR

Coaching Years: 11

Basic Coaching Philosophy: Enforce good fundamentals. Give athletes a solid base from which to start and then allow them to develop their own style for success. Respect, Dedication, Discipline and Accountability- must haves for a successful team.

How do you define or measure success? *I define success by the amount that my athletes grow – physically, socially and mentally. We want to turn out great softball players, but more importantly we want to turn out well-rounded young women who have learned the value of a challenge and want to continue to better themselves and their community.*

George W. Jones, Professional Instructor – St. Louis, MO

Accolades: Inducted into the St. Louis Sports Hall of Fame, Master of Ball Movement and Location, Pitching Coach for the St. Louis Hummers 1977-79 (Women's Pro League), Inducted into the Indiana ASA Hall of Fame, Midwest Major Pitcher 25 years, Professional Instructor for 23 years, Pitching Director / Instructor for numerous colleges

- *Through the years the students that followed George's teaching received many college scholarship offers. Through these same* *years the parents' savings are in excess of $3,000,000.00! George's videos can be found at*: **www.fastpitchvideos.com**

Interview with former All-American and Pro Amie Stewart

I was delighted to learn that Amie Stewart was willing to be interviewed for this publication. Amie is one of Fastpitch's greatest ambassadors, having excelled as a player and coach. Now coaching for the Corona Angels Red, she's been successful on so many different levels; here are some of her credentials:

- Played at ASA Nationals 16's – 18's
- She won ASA Nationals at 18u playing for Gordon's Panthers – Mays
- She attended UNLV and was a College All-American
- She also was voted All-Region as a DH and as a pitcher
- Played in the College World Series
- In 1995, achieved a 30-9 record and hit .325 with 10 home runs
- Named to the All-Tournament Team at the College World Series
- Played professionally for the Durham Dragons and the Tampa Bay Firestix.
- In 1997 participated in the Olympic Festival (Top 60 players in the nation)
- Was an ASA All-American in Women's Major
- In 1996, she pitched a three hit shutout defeating the Olympic Team 1-0, it was the team's only loss on their tour (64-1)
- She has served as both a high school as well as college coach
- Coached Gold in the summer going to nationals at 14u,16u, & 18u
- Placed the majority of her players at good schools on scholarships including: Notre Dame, Nebraska, Michigan State, Florida, Harvard, Arizona State, Georgia Tech, Ohio State, etc.

Amie, what has softball meant to you?

Softball has been my life since I started playing at 12. I love being an athlete and there are many rewards of this job. I got an education for free. I have traveled to almost every state and a few countries playing and it made me a better person. I learned to get along with others. It helped me become determined, aggressive, self motivated, and numerous other traits have been learned, which are great tools in life.

How did you first get involved as a player?

I was a gymnast my entire life but I started to become taller and bigger so I decided to take up softball. I was pretty good and I enjoyed playing. I started later than most girls these days; I started at age 12 playing in the Bobby Sox leagues and then moved up the ladder to travel ball, etc.

When did you realize that you had a special talent?

I guess my first year playing. I was an athlete so they made me a pitcher and I did well. I made All-Stars my first year playing and I just loved it so I worked hard with my parents at home to become better. My dad is very athletic so he helped me become better.

I was blessed with a first year coach that was a Men's Fastpitch player and he was a pitcher so he worked with me and taught me a lot about it. I was lucky to have him in my life during my first years. Bob Antrobus. He was amazing.

Who inspired you to play?

Honestly, probably my friends. I am very social and I loved being at the park with my friends. I loved beating the boys and striking them out. I guess it was a form of peer pressure, but I loved the game so it was a good thing. Then, I guess I motivated myself. I just liked playing. It made me a very confident person and I loved the attention. Ha…Ha… That's bad huh? But true. I loved doing things that I was successful at and softball was an amazing experience when I was younger. Larry Mays, my 18-under travel ball coach (Gordon's Panthers) inspired me to take it to a different level.

How is coaching different than playing?

It is very difficult to teach the things that are most important: work ethic, intuition, competitive nature, aggressive play, heart, motivation. Those variables come within an individual. I always had those traits so coaches didn't have to teach me these things. I wanted to win and had that desire. Just Saturday at practice, I asked my assistant coach how to teach this; it is so difficult. I want to get out there and play myself. I have to relate to my players as a player and that works. I have to keep them motivated with stories, situations, etc. Building confidence is the key.

What is your fondest memory as a player?

Wow, I have so many. I truly believe playing at the College World Series was my overall best experience but beating the US Olympic team comes close. The Series tournament is so much fun: Great fans, Great teams, ESPN games, Recognition. Playing against friends and having to forget they are your friends because you are trying to win games. It was an amazing experience. I love talking to the kids and signing autographs and the kids were the most amazing memories; there were so many kids. I loved press conferences. I also had a great bond with my teammates at UNLV and we did it together so it was gratifying. It was a fun tournament all around.

And, your fondest memory as a coach?

WOW, I have so many of these as well but it comes down to two tournaments. Winning the State Championships at the 16 under level in

2000 was a great experience. A lot of people did not believe we could be that strong of a team and I love for teams to underestimate me. I love being the "underdog" losing by 3 runs and 2 outs and we came back to win the game and the state title. People were shocked. We were shocked, but I knew that I had a great hitting team and anything is possible in a game.

The other tournament that was very special to me was the Colorado Fireworks tournament. There are over 100 teams and my team finished 5th that year. My players were mostly sophomores and juniors and I had at least 50 different colleges watching my team play in our final loss. We lost 1-0 in 9 innings on an outfield error against a team that had a majority of college freshmen but my sophomores and juniors held their own. It was awesome. My left fielder was so devastated by her error but even the fans and other team players were running over to her to console her. It was just a great game and nobody should have felt any regret. In the game prior to our final loss, we hit four home runs and blew out a strong Panther's Gold team. I remember my senior first baseman hit a back to back home run and she was sprinting around the bases jumping up and down. She was trying to get recruited, was panicking because the summer was over, and she hadn't committed and she was having the time of her life. It brought tears seeing them want something so much and going after it. It was awesome!

What was it like for you knowing that you had just pitched a shutout against the Olympic Team in 1996?

I really thought Leah O'Brien-Amico was going to win it for them because she hit me very well in college (she pinch hit with 2 outs and a runner on second). Getting past her was so great because I kept thinking; Leah is going to hit me. She has hit me so well in college and I don't know what to throw her right now. Thank goodness I had an awesome catcher that was older and had more experience and called an amazing game. I think I was more amazed that in going into the 7th inning, they only had one hit. I guess I never really thought about playing or winning so the situation just took over and at that point, you have nothing to lose; you just play to win. They should have beaten me. They were the best and I definitely was not at my top physical ability. It was just a fun situation.

I think that experience was a little surreal. My daughter was only 5-weeks old. I didn't think I was going to have to pitch but I am one to never give up and at least try something so I agreed to play. One of my best friends, Lori Harrigan, was walking down the dugout telling everyone I just had a baby and I was making them look stupid and I could hear her on the field. That actually just gave me more confidence but I was really just having fun in my hometown area. There were so many people at this game and they walked out quiet while our little rooting section of about 30 was jumping up and down. I just remember signing autographs and going home, sore as sore gets, and calling a few of my friends saying, "Guess what?' You're never going to believe this but I just beat the Olympic Team." Everyone was just ecstatic for me and it was an awesome game.

Now as a parent watching your daughter play, do you see the game differently than you did as a player?

Most definitely. Players are lazier, are less athletic, and boast a lot of demands these days. When I grew up, I watched and understood the game and earned my positions. I never made a coach guarantee anything but players now are spoiled and will just quit or go to another team. I see less loyalty than in the past and people give up rather than working harder to earn things. We were just athletes and played a lot of sports and did a lot of things. Now days, everyone focuses on one aspect of one sport and I feel sorry for them. I loved playing volleyball and basketball and going ice skating, etc. and I make sure my daughter has all of these other experiences to keep her well rounded and not bored. It seems most parents and players are so one dimensional when they need to understand every position because in college or the pros, etc, you just never know. Leah Amico is a great example. She was an awesome pitcher at Don Lugo in HS. She played P/1B at Arizona but was a starting outfielder on the Olympic team. Players need to have a general understanding of the game and every position because a coach has to do what is best for a team and utility players are a huge asset. I see parents and players say, "I feel I am a second baseman," and they work on second base but know nothing about the game. We thought more. Players these days seem less motivated than we were. It is all about appearance, them knowing it all, the "hype" and playing for the wrong reasons (i.e.: money, parents making them play, etc.) I think it is a reflection of professional sports in our times now. Generations have changed a lot.

For young people today, what is the best way for them to improve their skills and become the best players that they can be?

Obviously, working hard and putting the time and effort into practice is a must. Working on your own is huge. The mental game is huge and putting themselves in positive situations is important. I still believe doing a lot of different things to develop your skills as an athlete is important as well. In college, we did swimming, step aerobics, etc. to work on footwork, balance, endurance, etc. I love taking my daughter to gymnastics, dance, karate, ice skating, roller skating, playing bad mitten, croquet, etc. I believe all of these things help you become a better athlete and make it fun. I think players think too much instead of looking at the basic concepts. Players get into their heads too much instead of just doing what they do best and understanding you make mistakes. Parent support on good and bad days is necessary as well.

How can high school coaches help their talented athletes gain exposure with college programs?

Honestly, don't hate on the travel ball programs and help players find a good travel team. A lot of high school coaches worry about themselves and their programs and I understand that but travel ball is what is best for the players. Don't ban players from going to travel ball practice because it only makes your team stronger. Understand that college coaches cannot get to high school games as often because of their recruiting calendar. It is better to use a day watching forty teams at a tourney than two teams in a high school game. There will never be a lot of recruitment out of high school for softball. It just doesn't happen. Help them with their academics, have counselors helping to make sure they are taking their SAT's, taking the right classes, and passing because you can be the best player in the history of the sport but without an education, you won't get very far. Guide them in the right direction is my best advice.

Did you have any special training regimen that allowed you to reach your goals?

Nope. I actually was kind of lazy with my running and conditioning. I just didn't like to do it but I always worked very hard in practice, especially on my pitching and hitting. When I was first starting to pitch, my dad made me throw 200 pitches a day. Of course I was angry but now, it was the best thing he ever could have done. I always had great control, could throw a lot of games, and I didn't have to stress about anything except the number of pitches I threw. Repetition made me a great player and I wasn't freaking out in my mind about how perfect I had to be. I also believe in dry swings a lot for hitting. My 18-under travel ball coach had a chart for us that our parents had to sign that documented 100-200 swings three times a week. It made me stronger and I could work on good mechanics without getting frustrated at hitting the ball. Dry swings are awesome, especially in the mirror. I have my 10-under team do 50 and by May, they will be up to 100 swings twice a week. It develops strength.

Is there a magical age in which kids should start learning how to pitch?

I think to each is their own. I started late and still was very successful. I think starting early is great if parents don't burn them out. I think these days, kids start early so if your child loves it, let them start at whatever age they desire. I have 6-year olds that are doing well but parents need to remember that these kids are growing – learning to understand their bodies and abilities. I have a parent that demands perfection and the kid is only nine. This is unrealistic to me. I think kids are pushed too hard to develop things too quickly and they never master anything.

I have 10-under pitchers with five pitches and that is unrealistic to me. Give them a few to master before you mess them up. It is better to have three pitches that work anytime you want than five that don't work well. Realistically, I think that in 8-under, you should have a fastball; hit in and out targets, and start developing a change-up. By 10-under, master the change-up and start to develop another pitch, maybe two if they are very advanced. 12-under, master FB, Change and two pitches. 14-under, 16-under, 18-under, develop everything you have. Kids are pushed too hard at their ages.

How can a coach balance between pushing a player too much and not pushing her enough?

The best way is by getting to know your players. Some players take criticism well and you can get on them or yell. Some don't. Some need mental training while some have the desire and need physical training. Coaches need to understand that you cannot coach every kid the same way nor can you expect them to be the player you are. You have to find what makes each tick and treat them on an individual basis. Work on individual weaknesses to develop your players. Don't compare one player to the next because every person is different. Focus on a player's strength to build confidence.

How are prep players different today than when you participated in high school?

I went to Bellflower H.S. in Bellflower, Ca. I don't see much of a difference in prep than when I was in high school except the reasons we played. We just played to have fun and participate in high school activities because they were social. I believe players just are narrow minded and don't listen as much as we did. We trusted our coaches but unfortunately, a lot of the attitude comes from the parents. I think parents should let the kids play and have fun in high school and realize it is more social and competitive play is for travel ball. A lot of high school kids don't play travel ball but coaches push them like they are Olympic athletes. Understand that high school is a lot different in regard to ability.

How do players, best respond to their coaches?

By showing Respect, listening, taking something from every coach that teaches them and using it to their own individual advantage. Understand that your coach is going to make mistakes and you won't always agree with their decisions but treat a team like a family: Bond, Communicate, and Speak your mind in a respectful manor because a good coach will be able to tell you what they are thinking and justify their decisions, whether you agree or disagree. Don't hold negativity in because you will not be able to perform as well. There are a million decisions to make in a game. Some are risks and some are gut feelings but winners will take risks and winners will support the decisions and do their best to execute.

In closing, why have you chosen to remain active and involved with softball?

I love it. I love teaching kids and trying to give them the experiences I had being an athlete. It is very rewarding. I enjoy watching players go to college on scholarships because I understand that at work, nobody cares if you were an All-American. Get the education and life skills to carry you in anything you do. I enjoy watching my daughter have the fun and experiences I had. It keeps me young, smiling, and I will always love this sport.

Appendix

General Coaching Philosophy

By Jerrad Hardin
2003 Nebraska Coaches Association Softball Coach of the Year

Participating in a sport is an exhilarating experience; coaching a sport is an equally exhilarating moment. As a participant of many sports throughout my life, I always enjoyed the thrill of competition and the constant challenge to improve my skills. Fortunately I'm able to regenerate my passion for athletics through coaching. I feel very grateful for the opportunity to coach, and because of my feelings, I'm deeply committed.

Commitment may take many forms. However, commitment ultimately starts with a firm responsibility to the betterment of the student-athlete. Coaches can be extremely influential in athletes' lives and should understand this influence – and use it in an ethical, moral, and beneficial way. In a deeper sense, a coach has a responsibility to encourage an athlete to grow in ways that will help them be successful outside of the realm of athletics.

Athletics should be used as a tool to teach valuable life lessons. The vast majority of athletes will not follow a career path in athletics; however, the lessons learned through athletics will follow one through all walks of life. My passion to teach is as strong as my passion to coach. Every field and every court is a classroom that each coach can utilize to teach not only the skills of their respective sport, but also the lessons of life. Therefore, ultimate coaching bliss can not be measured by wins or losses, but instead by successes in and out of a sport.

Coaching Philosophy: Preparation

There really is no substitute for preparation. A coach should prepare athletes before the season, during the season, and in the off-season. It is a year-round process that requires a deep commitment to a vision the coach shares with the academic institution. A strong foundation can only be developed through complete preparation. Preparation has to involve the emotional, physical, and mental health of each athlete as well as the teaching of fundamental skills.

Preparation is not homogenous to merely the athlete; coaches are responsible for preparing themselves as well. Legendary UCLA basketball coach, John Wooden, has always stressed that coaches should be life-long learners. I faithfully believe this. Coaches should: read books, watch videos, talk with peers, engage in film analysis, register for clinics, observe games, and constantly search for ways to improve.

Coaching Philosophy: Practice

Administrative bodies will regulate the number of practice hours available for a team. Therefore, this time is precious and should not be wasted. Proper and thoughtful planning linked with strong discipline will make practices productive. I use a timer for every practice, and have a set number of minutes that I use during each drill. I want practice to be very organized with clear objectives that are expressed daily. Tangible team goals should be set for each practice. Creating a competitive atmosphere will allow the team to work together in problem-solving situations, which brings about a competitive edge as well as a spirit of unity and enthusiasm.

Coaching Philosophy: Games

Games provide competitors with a stage on which they can perform. I view games as opportunities: opportunities to improve, opportunities to participate, opportunities to have fun, and opportunities to achieve goals. Because of this belief I feel as though a coach and a team's approach to a game should focus on those aforementioned opportunities as opposed to focusing on the pressures of doing everything correctly. My belief is that practice allows you to be critical and judgmental regarding skills, whereas, games are intended to be viewed as opportunities to demonstrate learned skills. I'm not suggesting that a coach doesn't coach during competition, but a coach should allow his or her athletes to participate and grow through competition without bellowing over their every mistake. I see coaches who over-coach and never allow their players to grow. I often wonder if that's really any fun for the players involved. I want my athletes to enjoy competition and perform in competition without worries and pressures.

Coaching Philosophy: Characteristics of a Successful Coach

A coach needs to be steady. Competition brings out the best and worst in most of us. However, if a coach intends for his team to play consistently, then he needs to model consistency.

A coach needs to be himself. You cannot be someone else, and your kids will see through it if you attempt to be someone you are not. Be honest and truthful while allowing your athletes to see you for the person that you are.

A coach has a responsibility to be ethical and moral. A coach is in a tremendous position of leadership and is the ultimate role-model for his or her team. Therefore a coach should always keep ethics and morals in mind when making decisions.

Information Sheet

(Please print all information)

<table>
<tr><td rowspan="2">Name</td><td>Summer Team</td><td rowspan="2">Throw

R / L</td><td rowspan="2">Bat

R / L</td><td rowspan="2">Position #1</td><td rowspan="2">Position #2</td></tr>
<tr><td>Grade (2004-2005)</td></tr>
<tr><td rowspan="5">Please grade yourself in the following:

1 – Excellent
2 – Very Good
3- Good
4 – Average
5 – Not a strength

Being a good Teammate

1 2 3 4 5
Enthusiasm

1 2 3 4 5
Work Ethic

1 2 3 4 5
Hitting

1 2 3 4 5
Baserunning

1 2 3 4 5
Fielding

1 2 3 4 5
Throwing

1 2 3 4 5</td><td colspan="2">Contact Information:</td><td colspan="3">Experience:</td></tr>
<tr><td colspan="5">Briefly, please list what your individual goals are while participating as a member of the BW Softball Team:</td></tr>
<tr><td colspan="5">Briefly, please list what your team goals are while participating as a member of the BW Softball Team:</td></tr>
<tr><td colspan="5">What concerns, if any, do you have regarding the upcoming season?</td></tr>
<tr><td colspan="5">Do you have any special needs - or is there anything that yo feel I should know that will help me be a better coach for you?</td></tr>
</table>

Off-Season Sign-Up Sheet

COZAD SOFTBALL

Did you know that CHS has competed in the state softball tournament for four straight years?

Did you know that we have finished our season in the state championship game in three of the last four seasons?

Did you know that Cozad owns more state records in softball than any other team in any class?

Did you know that in the last three seasons six players went on or are going on to play college softball?

Did you know that no other team in any class has produced as many all-state players in the 1999 Class B Runner –Up *past four seasons as Cozad?*
2001 Class C State Champion 2002 Class C State Champion

Do you want to be part of the tradition?

Sign Up for Off-Season Batting Instruction (Only four per session)

8:30 – 9:30 p.m. Tuesday March 11th	**8:30 – 9:30 p.m. Tuesday March 18th**
1. 2. 3. 4.	1. 2. 3. 4.
8:45 – 9:45 p.m. Thursday March 20th	**8:30-9:30 p.m. Tuesday March 25th**
1. 2. 3. 4.	1. 2. 3. 4.

Lifting Routine

Target Areas

Upper Body	**Lower Body**	**Trunk**	**Cardio Wellness**
Shoulders Chest Arms	Hamstrings Quads Calves	Abdominals Hip Flexors	 Improve blood flow Expand lung capacity

Document all days of lifting – It's important that you don't miss or skip any part of your workouts.

Routine

<u>Circuit Training</u>

Week 1-4

Goal – Provide a foundation of strength through circuit training.

Weeks 1 & 2 – all lifts will be: 3x10
Weeks 3 & 4 all lifts will be: 3x12

Mondays & Thursdays

Always stretch before lifting.

Lifts:
<u>15 second rest between sets – 20 seconds between lifts</u> – stay on schedule!

Squats 3x10
Lunges 3x10
Calf Raises 3x10

Shoulder Press 3x10
Front Raises (shoulder) 3x10
Side Raises (shoulder) 3x10
Arm Curls 3x10
Triceps Pushdowns 3x10

30 Minute Cardio – (choice of jogging, bike, elliptical, or rowing)
200 Slow Crunches
Cool Down – Stretch Again.

Tuesdays & Fridays

Always stretch before lifting

Lifts

<u>15 second rest between sets – 20 seconds between lifts</u> – stay on schedule!

Squats 3x10
Leg Curls 3x10
Leg Extensions 3x10
Bench Press 3x10
Incline Press (chest) 3x10
Dumbbell Flies (chest) 3x10
Arm Curls 3x10
Triceps Pushdowns 3x10
200 Slow Crunches
10 Minute Cardio – (choice of jogging, bike, elliptical, or rowing)
Cool Down – Stretch Again.

<u>Strength Training</u> Goal – Produce a strong core for competition.

Weeks 5 & 6

Always stretch before lifting

Use heavier weights and lower reps. Make sure you lift enough that the last rep of each set is difficult to squeeze out.

M – F **(All 5 Days)**

Squats 3x6
Bench Press 3x6
Shoulder Press 3x6
Calf Raises 3x6
Triceps Extensions 3x6
Bicep Curls 3x6
200 slow crunches

Jump Rope 3 x 5 minutes
1 minute rest in between sets

6 -100 meter Sprints – 30 second rest in between

Important: Always seek the advice of professionals before engaging in a lifting routine.

Agility Drills
Power Skips

Skip 50 meters at maximum speed, with high knees.

Four Corner Drill

Create a box with cones (cones approximately 12 ft. apart). Do the following in 30 sec. Intervals:

- Touch all four corners as many times as possible in 30 seconds.
- Touch all four corners going in a diagonal pattern as many times in 30 seconds.
- Round each cone as many times in 30 seconds.
- Moving laterally, not crossing your feet, see how many times you can touch all four corners in 30 seconds.

Ladder Challenge

Using the length of the football field do the following:

- Run 10 yards stop, do 3 pushups
- Run 10 more stop, do 5 pushups
- Run 10 more stop, do 7 pushups
- Run 10 more, stop do 9 pushups
- Run 10 more, do 10 pushups
- Sprint out the last 50 yards

Catch Drills

1. Using a Nerf football play catch with a partner. Stand about 10 yards away from each other and move laterally with each other playing catch
- Variation: Start side by side – allow receiver to take off, and throw it over her head, forcing her to look back over her shoulder to make the catch.
- Variation: Receiver start on her back laying down, toss a ball in the air and so receiver has to get up and find the ball to try to make the catch.
- Variation: Start facing each other, toss the ball high and over the receiver's head, receiver must then turn and find the ball to try to make the catch.

2. Using a Frisbee play catch with a partner. Stand at variable distances from each other, focusing in on trying to catch it with your "catching" hand.

Tryouts

HITTING FOR AVERAGE

20 Pitches

***Ground balls that do not leave infield yield 0 pts.**
***Pop Flies that do not exceed outfield cones yield 0 pts.**
***Missed Swing results in a loss of pitch and yield 0 pts.**

20 Points Possible

HITTING FOR POWER

*** Will be determined by the total # of balls that exceed the outfield cones.**

20 Points Possible

SPEED

Home to Home Times

≤ 17 seconds = 10
≤ 18 seconds = 8
≤ 20 seconds = 6
≤ 22 seconds = 4
≤ 23 seconds = 2
≤ 24 seconds = 0

10 Points Possible

Fielding (Infield) from the SS area

20 Balls
5 Direct
5 Right
5 Left
5 Misc.

In order to get points for each, the player must cleanly field the ball & successfully make an accurate throw to 1st base.

20 Points Possible

Fielding (Outfield) from the CF area

20 Balls
5 Direct
5 Right
5 Left
5 Ground Balls

In order to get points for each, the player must cleanly field the ball and successfully hit the cutoff person.

20 Points Possible

Throwing Strength

Cones will be placed at different distances: 5, 10, 15, & 20 pt cones. Individuals must make a throw that surpasses each cone area on at least one hop to attain the point value. The ball must also land within a reasonable proximity to each cone of value.

We will score the best of 5 Throws.

20 Points Possible

Throwing Accuracy

10 throws are to be made from a designated area to the receiver standing at second base. The ball must hit the receiver in a position to make a tag, without her having to leave the base to catch the ball. No more than one bounce allowed.

10 Points Possible

Pre-Season Parent Letter

2002 Lady Haymaker Softball
2001 / 23-5 / State Champions

Dear Parent (s),

I welcome your interest in Cozad High School Softball. I'm excited about the upcoming season and **eager to work worth your daughter** during the 2002 campaign. One year ago we were talking about the opportunity of competing in a newly formed Class C. Now, we're talking about the opportunity of repeating as Class C State Champions!

Our softball program has quickly become **one of the top programs** in the state of Nebraska. Over the past four seasons we can be proud of accumulating 86 wins, multiple all-state awards, academic all-state selections, a myriad of state records, several invite championships, a district title, a state runner-up trophy (class B), and a state championship from a year ago.

This year **we've raised the bar** with our schedule in hopes of challenging our athletes. With the support of our administration we've made many changes to our schedule that includes the addition of Lincoln Southwest, Imperial, the Lincoln Southeast Invite, the North Platte Invite, and the Yutan Invite. In addition, familiar foes such as McCook, Lexington, North Platte, and Holdrege will remain on our schedule.

I'm expecting **twelve returning letter winners** for this year's team. In addition to the returning players I'm anticipating a number of freshmen as well. Of the returning players eight were every-day starters a season ago. Some preferences are awarded to returning players, however, positions are not given to players - they have to be earned every day in practice. A player's level of commitment, ability, and effort are used in evaluating who earns a starting role and playing time.

It is important that you as a parent know that we play at a very high level. We will be one of the top teams in our class. Our softball program competes at the **Varsity** level and every win or loss may dictate whether or not our team earns a trip to the state tournament. We as coaches will play who we feel are our best players. **Unfortunately we are not in a position where everyone gets to play or play in every game.**

We've had a great tradition with **parental support** and players who understand their roles. In part, that is why this program has been so successful. I look forward to your support, confidence, and understanding as we make another run at the State Tournament!

Thank You,

Coach Hardin

Please feel free to talk to visit with me during the season. However, I will not take any calls at home, nor are you welcome to visit with me at my home. If you have concerns, I will gladly talk with you about anything that concerns your daughter within a scheduled meeting. Please do not approach me before or after a game or practice if you have a conflict with how our staff operates, instead please follow the proper procedure and schedule a meeting

Daily Throwing Routine

Knee Throwing

- Set up at a 45 degree angle
- Isolated Wrist Snaps
- Tosses and Follow Through

Figure 8

- Move hand in figure 8-position – creating a long-loose movement that creates momentum and rhythm before throwing.

Back and Forth

- From a side-straddle position - rock back and forth, shifting the weight before throwing.

Catch and Throw

- Step to the ball with the right foot (turning it at a 45) catch it and throw it.

Loaded Throws

- Transfer weight to the backside, turn the shoulders, and throw. (Longer Distance)

Long Toss

- Partners should be equally matched so that maximum distance can be achieved. Tosses should be at a distance where the ball can only reach it's receiver on the bounce.

We want to maintain proper grip on the ball at all times, use proper footwork, and be focused with a minimum amount of chatter. This is done daily and it's treated as any other section of our drill work – it's not just a warm-up but an opportunity to improve throwing skills.

Daily Quick-Hitter Drills

Long-Short

Partners space themselves, all over the field, away from others. The tossing partner will toss one ball short, making the fielder come forward to make the catch – upon doing so she will flip it back to the tossing player and immediately start retreating to field a ball that is to be thrown long – over her head; players then switch.

Partner Ground Balls

Partners space themselves, on the infield, away from others. The drill starts by one player rolling the other a ground ball, upon fielding it cleanly she then rolls it back. It becomes a continuous drill. The drill starts slow, with balls tossed directly to one another, but quickly increases in speed and difficulty.

Four Person Rundown

Using four people, three will act as fielders and one will be the runner. We want to practice our rundown techniques of properly showing the ball, communicating and rotating.

Relay Throwing

Groups of three line-up and spread out across the field – the middle person will be the pivot person. We ask that she is always "open" to the throw with her hands ready, and that she catches and steps simultaneously to relay the throw. After four pivots we switch.

Coach's Call – Throwing

Players gather behind home, and choose groups, before sprinting out to each position when the coach says "Go!" Communication is essential, so that everyone knows where they are going. The coach then calls out any combination of throws in which the catcher initiates the drill with the first throw. (1st to 3rd to 2nd to Short to Home) The coach calls it once and it must be done without mistake. Upon completion the next group immediately hustles out to their positions and the drill repeats itself.

Sample Practice Plan

Thursday

3:45 – 4:05 - Stretch / Warm-up

Team	Ashley / Allie Erin / Tanya
4:05 - 4:10 Reaction Drill 4:05 – 4:10 Shorthop Drill 4:10 – 4:15 Ground Ball Fundamentals 4:15 – 4:20 Fly Ball Fundamentals 4:20 – 4:30 Sac Bunting	Ashley – North Cage * Pitching Warmup / Inside / Outside / Up / Down / Chage Erin – South Cage

4:30 – 4:40 Step / Hip / Swing

4:40 – 5:30 Machine BP

5:30 – 5:45 Team Infield / Outfield

"I learned to fight. I worked and studied it. If I got beat up or did something sloppy in the gym, I'd go home and work on it until I got it right. It was hard work, but I didn't want to just be good. I wanted to be the best."

~ *Thomas Hearns, Professional Boxer*

Coach Tom Spencer on HITTING

Know Your Strike Zone

If you want to be an intelligent batter and increase your productivity your **"hitting zone"** should theoretically change with the ball and strike count. For Instance:

One-Strike Count	The hitter's zone should be slightly larger than a no-count situation.
Two-Strike Count	The hitter's maximum zone should be recognized; you must protect yourself on corner pitches.
One-Ball Count	A smaller zone should be visualized by the batter. The hitter should be quite selective in the location of the next pitch.
Two-Ball Count	The hitter's zone should be very small. Only hit your "perfect" pitch.
Three-Ball Count	If allowed to hit it is the same as a two ball count.
Three-Ball—One Strike	The batter should picture your strike zone as in the two-ball count situation but not quite as selective.

Batting Slumps

Everyone should recognize that batting slumps are part of the game. Even top professional players experience the frustrations of slumps.

Here are the most common problems and a few suggestions that may help you.

1. *Not Making Contact*

   The most common reason for this is you are just not seeing the ball all the way in. Make certain that your front shoulder and head stay in.

2. *Hitting all ground balls*

   This is usually an indication that you are swinging too early. Concentrate on waiting longer for the pitch. Think of hitting the ball up the middle will also help. Just as the pitcher is releasing the ball do a slight inward turn of your front shoulder

3. *Hitting a lot of pop-ups*

   It's usually caused by swinging late or by upper-cutting. Open your stance just a little and choke up on the bat. REALLY concentrate on swinging down.

Where should you be making contact with the ball?

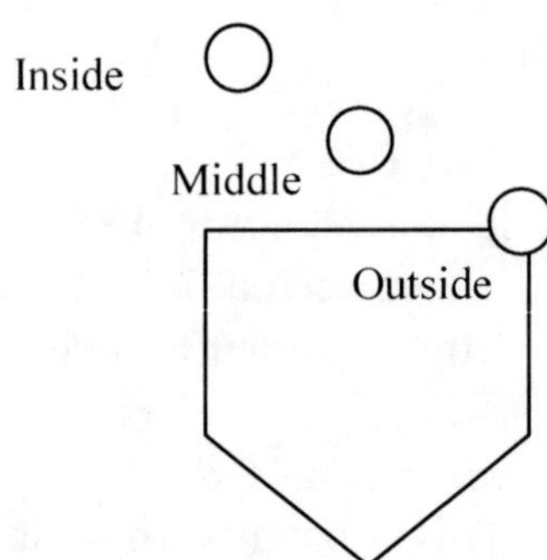

A hitter's point of contact should be directly relevant to pitch location. For instance, on an inside pitch, a hitter's contact point will be much farther in front of the plate than that of an outside pitch. Having knowledge of this will optimize results when executed properly. For coaches, it's important that we teach contact points and properly emphasize them in the drills that we do.

Advice for Being a Better Hitter:

- When you step to the plate be focused and determined to hit. Go up to the plate thinking "Hit". Hitting is as much a mind-set as anything else.

- Be extremely disciplined with a strong work ethic toward practice. You must commit your training into muscle memory. That's why we may do so well with soft toss, tee-work, and the cage, but struggle against live pitching. You have to commit your training into muscle memory to be effective. That means lots and lots of swings.

- Be open to new ideas and change. You have to be willing to constantly grow as a player, so take any new advice you can get.

- When practicing keep all of your fundamentals in mind, and no matter how poorly you are hitting the ball, continue to keep yourself focused, not allowing yourself to develop bad habits. It is easy to stray away from what you're supposed to be doing when things aren't going well, but you only go backwards when your practice habits are bad.

Captain's Application

Name _______________________ Grade _____________

Honors:

Current Classes: GPA:

1. What qualities do you feel a good team captain must possess?

2. Would you describe yourself as a vocal leader or one who leads by example? Why?

3. Please provide us with someone that you look up to, who you feel is a positive role-model.

4. What role do you think a team captain should perform?

5. Describe what being selected as a team captain would mean to you.

Upon completion of this application, please return it with three letters of recommendation and a completed essay on why you think you would be a good team captain to Coach Hardin before January 15th to be considered as a candidate.

2003 Lady Haymaker Softball
2001 / 23-5 / State Champions
2002/ 38-6 / State Champions

Rules are given to players to serve as a guideline of expectations. If the set rules are followed by everyone, then you will find this softball season to be very enjoyable.

Team Rules

1. **Don't do anything that would embarrass yourself, your team, or your family**. If you think you're doing something that you could potentially get into trouble for if caught, then chances are you shouldn't be doing it.

2. Show respect to others that are talking – **Look them in the eye and give them your full attention**. If you have something to say, listen to the person talking and wait until it's your turn to talk.

3. Display team unity at all times. **"I go, we go"** – There shall be no individual or group effort to make any one person or any group of individuals feel not a part of the team.

4. No player should discipline another. That's my job. Make me aware of the situation and it will be handled accordingly. You may not see how the situation is handled, so please **don't judge how I do my job** and create an internal problem.

5. Players must be on time and prompt, there will be **no tolerance** for players being tardy or missing practice for a predetermined unexcused reason.

6. Many of you have played softball for a long time, and have had the opportunity to work with many different coaches. I think that's a valuable asset. However, **you will not openly question**

anything that we do. There are many different ways to play this game, and you will not be allowed to question how this coaching staff chooses to play. In order to be successful, you have to believe in what you're being taught and do it with 100% effort.

Any interpretation that suggests a violation of the above team rules will be handled appropriately by the coaching staff and school administration if needed. Consequences may include, but are not limited to, a suspension regarding play to a permanent dismissal from the team.

Your standing on this softball team will be determined by:

1. Your attendance and readiness for practice, study nights, functions and games.
2. Your social behavior away from softball.
3. Your ability to be a team player.
4. Your participation in all softball activities.
5. Your academic performance.
6. Your willingness to accept and follow the rules that have been outlined.

COZAD LADY HAYMAKER SOFTBALL RULES AND EXPECTATIONS FOR PLAYERS

GENERAL

All players are expected to show respect at all times for the entire coaching staff.

- Accept what is being taught to you.
- Address all coaches in a respectful manner.
- Understand that your coaches are there because they want to be there to help you.

All players are expected to work together to achieve a common goal.

- Accept all of your teammates and do not single any one person or group out.
- Encourage and be supportive of your teammates at all times.
- Understand that we are all in this together.

All players are expected to be positive role models on and off the court.

- Accept the fact that children will look up to you and lots of eyes will fall on you.
- Conduct yourself as a model citizen off the court, and display good sportsmanship on the court.
- Understand that the image you portray is important.

PRACTICE

- Players are expected to be at practice on time and ready to go when practice begins, being late will not be tolerated and will result in a loss in playing time and team standing.
- Any negative actions in practice including but not limited to the following will result in an automatic ejection from practice without warning: profanity, anger, negative attitude, talking back to any of the coaches
- Lack of effort, enthusiasm, or togetherness will not be tolerated.
- Have fun.

<u>*GAMES*</u>

- Adhere to deadlines, proper dress code, and other game policies that may be mentioned. Results of non-compliance will result in lack of playing time or if it becomes a repetitive problem it may be handled in a different way.
- Always conduct yourself properly at other schools, the bus, and places to eat.

The coaching staff will interpret all of the aforementioned.

For issues concerning other matters not mentioned, the activity handbook will be applied.

State Tournament Itinerary

<u>Wednesday Morning</u>

8:00 a.m. : State Tournament Send-Off
8:45 a.m. : Leave Cozad

1:00 p.m. : Practice at Creighton
4:15 p.m. : Check-In at the Red Lion Inn

5:45 p.m. : Leave for the Banquet
6:30 p.m. : Banquet

7:30 p.m. : Return to the Red Lion
8:00 p.m. : Team Movie

10:30 p.m. : Lights Out

7:00 a.m. : Wake – Up
7:45 a.m. : Leave for Seymour Smith
8:00 a.m. : Begin Warm-Up
8:45 a.m. : Team Picture
9:10 a.m. : Round of Infield on the Main Field
9:30 a.m. : Opening Ceremonies
10:00 a.m. : v. Wahoo
12:00 p.m. : Take Infield
12:30 p.m. : Game 2

Room Assignments

Room 1	Room 2	Room 3	Room 4	Room 5
Pook Ashley Erin	**AJ** Miranda Allison	**Pede** Tasia Kim	**Val** Brooke Katie Tanya	**Jenny** Saranne Kylee Rachel

The person in **bold** is responsible for governing their room. They also are in charge and responsible for the room.

Kim Terry will be our female sponsor – you may also refer to her in appropriate situations.

Keys & Comparisons

Facts about Elkhorn: 25 – 6

Average Runs Allowed Per Game – 1.1 **Cozad** Averages – 1.9 or 1.01 earned
Average Runs Scored Per Game – 5.7 **Cozad** Averages – 8.3

Most runs allowed in one game this year – 5, Ralston **Cozad** – 13, Holdrege
Most runs scored in one game this year – 17, Nebraska City **Cozad** – 19, S.V.

Losses - Blair, Ralston, Omaha Gross, Valley, Fremont, Norris
Cozad - McCook (2), Holdrege, GINW, North Platte, Lexington

Six starters return from last year's team that lost to Cozad 3-2 in extra innings.

Key Players:

JR. P. - 191 Ks, 162 innings ERA - .56

SR. SS - 6 doubles, 5 triples

JR. 3B - 6 doubles

No Common Opponents

Keys for Cozad

Offensive

- Lay off of pitches high and away.
- Look for her first pitch to be a good one.
- Be very proficient in the short game.
- Aggressive on the bases.

Defensive

- Limit the amount of pitches we have to throw.
- Play error-free.
- Don't give up the big play.
- A shutout is needed.

Lincoln Northeast

3 Pitchers:
19– Senior Lefty – Very slow and hittable
31– Righty – Dropball / Fastball – Descent Speed – Generally Outside
1– Sophomore – Relies purely on her drop ball – Move up vs. her

Offensively – As a team they are free-swingers
Fr. *21* has great hands and can crush it – Must Change speeds v. her.
Fr. *12* has an inside out swing – Will try to hit to right field
2 and *4* – Will look to bunt for hits

Defensively – Average
Left side with the SS and 3B is real solid.
CF has a great arm.
The Catcher has a quick release and a good arm – not great.

Papillion Lavista

Probable Pitcher – 14

Scouting Report:

Very Good Pitcher
Five Pitches:

- Good Rise
- Likes to Control the Pace – Make sure you're in control as a hitter – Step Out and frustrate her.

Defensive Key – Be very good against the slap. Be heads up for aggressive baserunning and trick plays.

Top Offensive Players – 15, 12, 2, 33, 3,

3 and 33– Very Good once they get on. – Infielders will need to get rid of it quick.
15, 12, 2 – Will hit for Power. – Outfielders need to adjust back.

Overall approach to the tournament

- Have fun! Always keep your head up – that keeps you in it
- Always hustle and be sharp! We're too good to be sloppy and lazy
- Never ever give up no matter what the score! Winning or Losing

Scouting Form

Opponent _______________

Game ______________________ **Date**________________

Score ______________________

Top Players	Strengths	Swing Flaws	Defensive Alignment

Slappers : **Bunters: Speed:**

Pitchers

Name	Best Pitch	Most - Used

0-0 Count	0-1	0-2	1-2	2-2	3-2

1-0	2-0	2-1	3-1	Tip Offs

Pace: **Rhythm:**

Grips: **Mannerisms:**

____ Name ______________

	Pitch Sequence							Result / Notes
1st								
2nd								
3rd								
4th								

____ Name ______________

	Pitch Sequence							Result / Notes
1st								
2nd								
3rd								
4th								

____ Name ______________

	Pitch Sequence							Result / Notes
1st								
2nd								
3rd								
4th								

____ Name ______________

	Pitch Sequence							Result / Notes
1st								
2nd								
3rd								
4th								

Hitting Chart

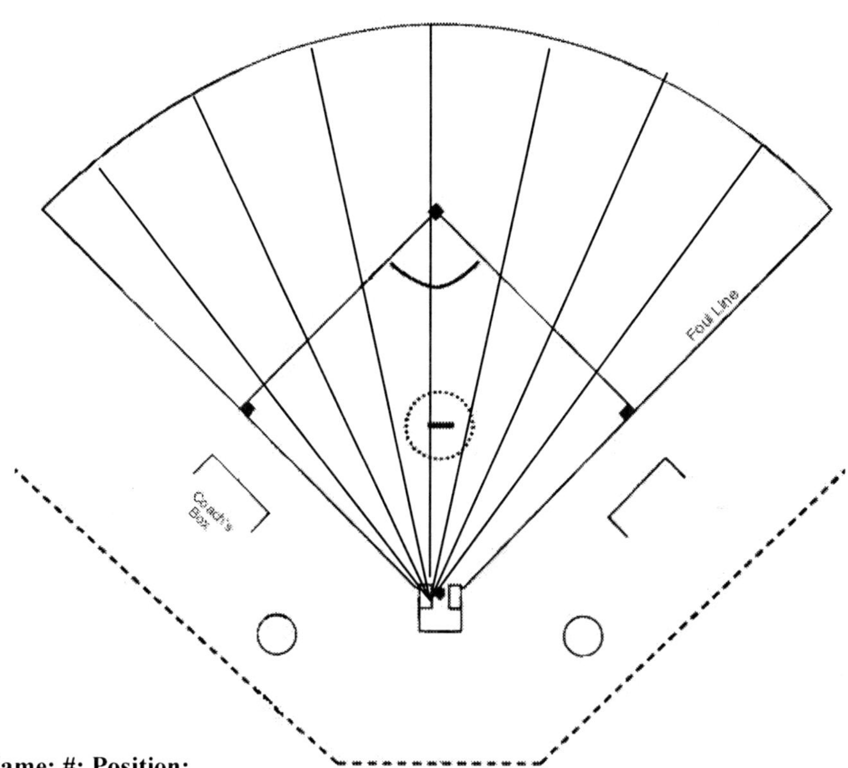

Name: #: Position:

Plate Appearance	**Pitch Hit**	**Result**	**Strikeout Pitch**
1.			
2.			
3.			
4.			

Symbols: G – Ground Ball F – Fly Ball L – Line Drive
X – Out H – Hit

CHS SOFTBALL Quiz

NAME ________________________

Pitching Signs

1 =

2 =

3 =

4 =

5 =

Fist =

Five Finger Wiggle =

Hitting Signs

Indicator =

Bunt =

Slap =

Take =

Steal =

If you are a batter how do we protect our runner stealing?

What do you do to acknowledge your received a sign?

Fly Ball communication

A fly ball is hit between the Outfield and Middle Infielders how is it handled:

Printed in the United States
116581LV00002B/144/A

9 781591 139348